For my dear friend, Helen Badge
(1940–2011)

'If I had a flower for every time
you made me smile, I'd be walking
in an endless garden.'
— *Anonymous*

The
Edible Balcony

How to grow fresh food in a small space
plus 60 inspiring recipes

Indira Naidoo

Photography by
Alan Benson

LANTERN
an imprint of
PENGUIN BOOKS

CONTENTS

THE EPIPHANY

I was very much a City Girl.

My world consisted of cars, gridlock, pollution, television studios, office towers, fluorescent lights, noisy bars, restaurants, manicures, drycleaners, high-rise apartments, concrete and steel. I could easily go a week without my feet touching a blade of grass, my hand brushing up against the bark of a tree or my nose taking in the scent of a flower. I was about as far removed from nature as any human being on the planet could be.

My food was packaged and convenient – free of dirt, grit or blemishes. Where it came from before it landed on my supermarket shelf, I didn't know, and I cared even less. When it came to meal preparation, minimising time had become far more important than maximising flavour. Like many time-poor urban professionals, even 'ten-minute' meals took far too long.

As a card-carrying member of Generation Jet-set, my urban jungle may have triumphed over the environment, but deep down I was slowly beginning to question what sort of world it had delivered. In this burgeoning age of green, organic and natural, had I become a perfect candidate for – how would the North Korean government put it – re-education?

My motivation to reconnect with my inner hunter/gatherer came to me as most of my epiphanies do – when I was hungry. I was shopping at a farmers' market in Sydney, when a stallholder offered me one of his cherry tomatoes to sample. I thanked him and popped it in my mouth distractedly, thinking about what I was going to buy for lunch.

The flavour detonation that followed stopped me in my tracks.

It was like no tomato I had ever tasted – sweet and full-flavoured, its thin, delicate skin wrapped around a juicy, fruity centre. It was how I remember tomatoes tasting from my childhood. I spun around on my heels and made a beeline back to the stall.

'That tomato was delicious,' I said enthusiastically. 'Where did you get it?'

'I grew them myself,' said the stallholder.

'Really?' I said, incredulously. 'But why does it taste so good? I try to buy fresh organic tomatoes all the time but they don't taste like that.'

'It's an heirloom variety that hardly anyone grows anymore. Commercial growers aren't interested in them because they don't store or transport well. You need to eat them on the day they're picked,' he said. 'If you keep the seeds, you can grow some yourself,' he said.

'But I live in an apartment,' I said, perplexed.

'Do you have a balcony and some sunlight?'

'Well... yes,' I said.

'Then it'll be easy,' he said.

What an extraordinary idea. Could it be that simple to grow my own food, even though I lived in a thirteenth-floor apartment with no garden? I bought a bag of his tomatoes and rushed home to transform them into a simple tomato and basil pasta sauce for lunch.

It was a meal I will never forget. The flavours were ethereal. What other home-cooked, Michelin-starred delights was I missing out on because my store-bought tomatoes were sub-standard? I realised I had put up with flavourless tomatoes for too long. Right there and then I resolved to try and grow my own.

Little did I know that one tiny tomato was to be the catalyst for a food-gardening obsession that would change my life...

SETTING UP YOUR BALCONY GARDEN

DIGGER'S

PEA GREENFEAST

The traditional peas for shelling. Great flavour.
Grow up support.

Pisum sativum
Harvest in 80 days
Sow direct in Spring
Grow ☀ ◐
Type HARDY ANNUAL
Size 120cm — 10cm
Id SU910
Best before Dec 2011
Germination 97 %
Seed count 90
Product code S165
Pkd NZL2009/CANSEED27482
Retail $3.30 Club $2.75

Y ou want to do what?!' This was my husband, Mark's, response when I mentioned my idea to him one morning over a cuppa.

'I want to grow some tomatoes and a few other vegetables on our balcony,' I repeated, trying to sound upbeat but thinking this conversation wasn't going too well.

'We'll have fresh herbs and vegies on tap. And maybe some of our friends will be inspired to do the same,' I said feebly.

'But we live in an apartment. On the thirteenth floor, for Christ's sake! In the middle of a metropolis! I don't want the place overrun with triffids,' he added, somewhat melodramatically I thought.

'The place won't be *overrun*,' I said, slightly annoyed and summoning that authoritative newsreader tone I often deploy to get myself out of scrapes. 'I'll draw up a plan that will still leave us with enough room on the balcony for the barbecue, the bench, the table and our deckchairs. The plants won't get in the way at all.'

There was no way he was going to buy that.

'What about the view?' Mark asked, convinced our harbour vistas would disappear behind a green jungle of knotted roots, leaves and branches.

'Well, of course *some* of the views will be obscured, but if you lean over the balcony on the eastern side and crane your neck around the corner, you'll still get some water glimpses,' I said brightly, sounding like a Potts Point real estate agent.

'You really do come up with some doozies, Naidoozies,' he said, and as soon as I heard that familiar, endearing phrase, I knew he was beginning to warm to the idea.

'There will need to be rules governing all of this – very definite rules,' he said in a headmasterly tone. 'And you'll have to grow some salad ingredients as well.' Mark loved his fresh salads.

'Of course,' I said, barely able to control my rising excitement. I couldn't believe he had acquiesced without me even having to resort to my lower-lip pout!

Well, that was the husband sorted. Now I just needed some ground rules . . .

THE RULES

Rules are made to be broken. But I was sensible enough to realise that setting up some guiding principles from the outset would keep the hubby happy and give this project some much-needed structure. I convinced Mark that I would do some thorough, independent research before the first seed was planted. So, like any other journo would, I googled it.

With the recent resurgence of the 'grow-your-own' movement that convinced even the Obamas to turn part of the White House lawn into a vegie plot, I was confident it wouldn't take me long to find what I was looking for. However, I soon realised that a gardening project on the scale I was contemplating had never been attempted on a high-rise balcony – or at least it had not been documented. Did that mean I was charting new territory, or turning into a nutter? (That's a rhetorical question, by the way.)

While there were some helpful websites about

✱ I screamed like a banshee whenever I saw a cockroach; how was I going to squash a caterpillar?

container gardening and growing vegetables in small spaces, there wasn't a lot of advice about growing food on balconies. This dearth of information seemed odd, given that two-thirds of Australia's twenty-one million people live in cities and, of the 7.9 million households living in private dwellings (2005–06 Australian Bureau of Statistics figures), 11% of those live in flats, units or apartments – many of these with balconies, I assumed. I was going to have to fly blind on this one.

So, what did the parameters for this experiment need to be? What could I do and what couldn't I do? After fruitless searches of websites, reference books and garden centres, I eventually went to the one source I should have consulted at the beginning – gardening guru, Peter Cundall, now retired from television and heroically fighting to save endangered wilderness in Tasmania.

'Start small,' he said. 'Don't set the bar too high. Don't be too prescriptive; you want to be encouraged to grow your own food, not put off. Share the ups and downs; that's reality. Read and study everything you can. Take advice. Then put it into practice. You'll weep at your failures, but gloat over your successes. Your relationship will be tested. You'll lose friends, and make new ones. Good luck and never give in. Growing your own food is a magnificent addiction; that's why I'll never stop fighting for the environment.'

Peter's wise words were a reality check. Did I really want to do this? Did I have what it took? It sounded worse than becoming a parent for the first time. Plants were needy – they required regular watering, fertilising and pest patrols. I screamed like a banshee whenever I saw a cockroach; how was I going to squash a caterpillar? Would my plants start dictating my life? What would I do when my work took me interstate or overseas? Suddenly, fingers of doubt grabbed my gut and squeezed hard. What made me think I could do this? I wasn't a gardener. I'd grown a few herbs before with mixed success, but that was all.

I desperately needed some air. I stepped out onto the balcony and took a long, deep breath, taking in the space as if for the first time. I looked at the bare tiles and the concrete walls, and in their place I pictured a lush, verdant food garden, filled with fruits and aromas, foliage and flowers. I imagined picking vegetables straight from the bush, or snipping off some fresh herbs for a meal. I thought about the wondrous smells and tastes, and the satisfaction of knowing I had grown it all by myself on a small, urban balcony. I remembered the heady flavour of that heirloom tomato I had tasted at the farmers' market, and all my niggling doubts evaporated on the spot. I was going to do this. I was going to create an edible balcony. And these were the rules I settled on.

Rule 1 You can't grow everything you eat, but you can eat everything you grow.

Rule 2 Conduct a site assessment, taking into account the amount of space and sunlight available and the prevailing climate, and assess how much time you can reasonably devote to the garden, before planting anything.

Rule 3 Start with a few simple herbs and greens, then move onto vegetables when you are more confident.

Rule 4 Try and use something you have grown yourself in every meal you cook at home.

Rule 5 Try to use only organic and chemical-free fertilisers and pest-control methods.

Rule 6 Be water-wise.

Rule 7 Use recycled products wherever possible.

Rule 8 Only grow what you like to eat.

Rule 9 Share your produce with family, friends and neighbours.

Rule 10 Don't be fanatical about these rules.

In addition to these rules, I put together a time-management plan which ensured that – after the initial set-up – I only needed to commit ten minutes a day to maintain my plants; anything more would have seemed like a chore. These ten minutes, either first thing in the morning or at night after work (possibly with a G & T in hand), would be spent watering, fertilising, dealing with pests and on general maintenance such as weeding and pruning. Minimum input with maximum reward was going to be my mantra.

WHY GROW YOUR OWN FOOD?

As we grab our briefcases, rush out the door, jump in the car and join the traffic snarl to our offices, it's hard to imagine that, not that long ago, most of us used to be farmers. We were all once involved, in some way, in growing our own food; intimately associated with the land and totally reliant on weather patterns. I'm sure you all remember this from history class, but I'm not just talking about medieval times. This was what life was like in the early 1900s, when most people lived in rural communities. And even in a highly urbanised nation such as Australia, almost everyone had a vegetable patch. So how, in just over 100 years, have we moved so far away from our farming roots? Now the only thing most of us are any good at growing is the mould on our out-of-date vegies in the fridge.

The move to the cities The reason we stopped farming was because we abandoned village life for the lure of the big city. In 1900, there were 1.5 billion people in the world, and around fourteen cities with more than one million people. Fast-forward to the present day, and the world's population has quadrupled to over six billion. There are now 400 cities with more than one million people. The vast majority of us living in industrialised countries now reside in big cities where, for the most part, our daily needs are met by a large, unseen infrastructure. Our cities and sprawling suburbs now cover the very market gardens that used to feed us. Most of our food has to be shipped, flown or trucked in, leaving us clueless about where it has come from or how it was grown.

This disconnect is having dangerous ramifications; we just have to switch on the television news to see the fallout. We are bombarded with media stories about mad cow disease, milk-substitute scandals, pesticide poisoning, childhood obesity and soaring grocery prices. The floods of 2011 decimated 10% of the country's fruit and vegetable produce. $500 million worth of perishables was lost and prices of mangoes, capsicums and tomatoes skyrocketed (*The Sydney Morning Herald*, 24 January 2011). The devastation highlights how dependent we are on commercially grown crops, such as lettuce, that many of us could easily grow ourselves.

* When a day at the office leaves you depleted, just ten minutes spent in the garden can quickly bring life back into focus.

Taking control Growing food on your inner-city balcony is clearly not the answer to all these maladies. But I wondered if it could give me a renewed sense of control and stewardship over my food and my environment, and, in these straitened financial times, save me some money along the way? I'm clearly not alone. The appeal of growing-your-own, or at least the theory behind it, seems to be universal. It's because the results are tangible: you get to eat what you grow. And even a small vegetable plot can save you a few hundred dollars on your annual grocery bill, and give you a certain degree of food security – that is, having access to affordable, safe food. It also serves our need to be close to nature; we find it restorative and relaxing. When a day at the office leaves you depleted, just ten minutes spent in the garden discovering a new shoot or a fruit bud can quickly bring life back into focus. It heals us.

But could I keep channelling the Dalai Lama even after a vicious wind gust had destroyed my pampered seedlings? I was about to find out . . .

The back story

Good on ya, Mum I was luckier than some – I grew up with parents who cooked every day and grew their own vegetables. Every meal contained fresh garden produce combined with the exotic spices that form the basis of South African–Indian cuisine. Some dishes would take my mother all day to prepare; a lamb biryani layered with lentils, spicy lamb and fragrant saffron rice, steamed in the oven for several hours; tangy fish curry scented with tamarind, curry leaves and smoky eggplant; braised paprika-flecked potatoes with garden-fresh peas, mint and coriander. Very little of what we ate was processed. What appeared on our dinner plates looked very much like what it had been when it was alive – fish, meat and plants. Typically, though, like most children, we always wanted what our friends were eating. The care and effort that went into our nutritional, home-cooked meals meant little to us. The culinary highlights of our childhood were instead the frozen fish fingers we had on a Friday night or the bucket of Kentucky Fried Chicken enjoyed after a Sunday drive, when our weary parents eventually gave in to our pestering. Frozen dinners and fast food when sumptuous Indian banquets were on offer? I shudder at the memory. Sorry, Mum.

Convenience culture To modern-day households, I know my childhood sounds like a John Howardesque, white-picket-fence, Pollyanna fantasy. A parent at home all day! Elaborate home-cooked meals! Space to plant a veggie patch *and* the spare time to tend to it! Wake up and smell the roses, Indira, no-one lives like that anymore, I hear you say. I know, I know. These days, most of us are just trying to keep our heads above water. What with global financial meltdowns, huge mortgages, rising interest rates, both parents working and long commutes to the office, what we cook and eat has plummeted to almost rock-bottom on our list of priorities. We need our food to be fast, fuss-free and filling, so we've relegated the onerous responsibility of feeding ourselves to the trillion-dollar food industry. Our food now arrives via scanners, conveyer belts or drive-throughs, packaged in styrofoam, cardboard boxes and plastic bags, scrubbed, glistening and blemish-free: not much tastier than the packaging it comes in. This so-called convenience food has often been achieved at the expense of flavour, nutrition, our health and the environment.

I want it now!

I think we've forgotten what real food tastes like. Produce is no longer grown for flavour but for how well it will store and survive transportation. What makes a tomato juicy and tasty is sometimes also the very quality that makes it highly perishable.

When we select our produce at the supermarket, we often look for perfection: apples that look like they've fallen from the pages of a toddler's alphabet book, not off the branch of a tree. Most of us know that apples are often polished with wax to make them super-shiny, but how often do we remind ourselves of that?

Bring back seasons Fruit and vegetables have the best flavour when they are in season. This also makes them cheaper. But how many of us know, for example, what is the best time to eat strawberries, when they're available all year-round? We rarely question the fact that we can eat *anything* we want, *whenever* we want. We think this is progress. Our grandparents would reel in horror. Growing and eating according to the seasons, as they did in their day, ensured bigger crops and less need for chemicals and fertilisers, and maximised the nutritional content of the harvest. Sure, they could only eat cherries once a year, but for the rest of the time there were other berries to feast on that held their own allure. And boy, did they look forward to cherry season! Much of this makes sense when we take time to stop and think about it. But our lives are so furious with activity, so cluttered with tasks, that we rush through the supermarket checkout after work, often with screaming kids in tow, in a stressed-out daze. And this distraction is just what the food industry is banking on.

Our jet-setting vegies

The next time you're in your local supermarket, take a closer look at the fruit and vegetables packed on those black plastic trays in the refrigeration section and you'll see that, surprisingly, many of them haven't been grown in Australia at all. In fact, some have come from the other side of the world. You can find oranges from California, bananas from Indonesia and dates from the Middle East. A study by Melbourne's Centre for Education and Research in Environmental Strategies found that a typical basket of goods bought in a Melbourne supermarket had travelled a staggering 70 000 kilometres. That's equivalent to two round-the-world trips. Don't you hate it when your vegies are better travelled than you are?

Food miles This is the term coined to describe how far our food has travelled to get to us. Many people use this as a guide to measure the environmental impact of a product. The theory goes that the further a food product has been transported, the more food miles it racks up and the more harmful the impact it has on the environment through greenhouse gas emissions and the burning of fossil fuels. Food miles, though, should not be the only way we assess the environmental impact of what we buy. We need to also factor in how much energy is used to grow (including hothousing, fertilising and watering), package and store the produce. Sometimes these processes can have a more damaging impact on the local ecology than freight. One thing you can say with certainty is that the food miles you rack up from walking to your balcony garden and pulling out a few spuds will be infinitesimal by comparison.

How fresh is this really?

Given that our produce has often travelled great distances, you probably wouldn't be surprised to learn that it's not as fresh as it would have been had it been picked straight from the garden. You *would* be surprised to know that some of the produce we buy couldn't be classed as 'fresh' at all. Some fruit and vegetables, such as grapes and strawberries, are already at least two weeks old by the time we put them in our trolleys, and some apples have been stored for more than a year (*choice.com.au*). Fruit and vegetables continue to lose their nutrients after they've been harvested, especially green leafy vegetables. Worse still, when you take your produce home, the nutritional depletion doesn't stop. *Choice* research found that the broccoli they sampled had lost half its vitamin C content after being stored in a home refrigerator for a week. The nutritional boost we think we're getting from that limp bunch of spinach, for example, is sadly far less than if we bought a box of snap-frozen spinach. Even some canned vegetables have more nutrients than their poor-quality fresh counterparts.

Bitter taste in your mouth? And while we're fretting over nutrients, we should also be vigilant about pesticide residues. There are more than 300 registered pesticides that can be used on Australian-grown fruit and vegetables. A 2003 Australian Total Diet Study by Food Standards Australia New Zealand (FSANZ) found the highest level of pesticides to be present in lettuce and strawberries. While there is no conclusive evidence to show that the very low levels of pesticides permitted in our produce could be harmful to our health, many consumers don't want to take the risk. The reason many people switch to organic and home-grown is so they can be safe in the knowledge that their vegetables are pesticide-free.

Time to start smelling the zucchini flowers

The combination of high-calorie processed foods and a lack of fresh fruit and vegetables in our diet, plus an increasingly sedentary lifestyle, is slowly killing us. Australia's obesity epidemic now costs the nation $56 billion dollars a year in direct healthcare and other care costs (*The Sydney Morning Herald*, 1 March 2010). It's been estimated that one in five Australian children are overweight or obese. There have been dire predictions that today's generation of children may be the first generation to die before their parents.

The solutions to these 'lifestyle' diseases are multi-faceted. But growing some of your own food is a good way to reconnect with plants and the critical role they play in our diets. And it's good to start young. Here in Australia, Stephanie Alexander's Kitchen Garden Foundation is tackling the problem head-on. This ambitious scheme teaches schoolkids how to grow and cook healthy, nutritious food and gets them active at the same time. At the time of writing, there were 139 schools across the country participating in the scheme.

A free workout Growing your own food, even on a small balcony, is damn good exercise. Lugging containers and bags of potting mix, bending, planting, watering, weeding – it certainly gets the heart rate up. Regular garden chores can burn anywhere from 120 to 200 calories per half-hour, depending on the intensity of the activity. So throw out your lycra and slip on your floppy hat, your Crocs and your trackie daks, and join me in the garden.

ENJOYING THE SPOILS

Of course, the main motivation for starting a food garden is to be able to enjoy the fruits of your labour. Being surrounded by pots brimming with fresh produce will be a source of endless inspiration. It will encourage you to throw together more home-cooked meals and to eat what is in season. The recipes in this book were all created with at least one ingredient from my edible balcony – and in some cases, I can proudly boast as many as four were used!

EMBRACE YOUR BALCONY

Let's cut to the chase – most balconies are pretty uninspiring spaces. They're usually a storage area for the clutter that won't fit in your apartment. The Aussie balcony is the great unsung hero of urban life. Whether yours is big or small, shaded or sunny, solid or flimsy, it's the only backyard you've got so maybe it's time you started treating it like one.

Before you start, make sure you check the balcony regulations with your landlord, your building's strata committee or your body corporate. Every building is different and the additions that may be acceptable to one could be a definite no-no to another.

Size matters

Look at your balcony as you would a potential lover. Size it up objectively. Look at its curves and dimensions. What are its strengths, and what are its failings? Would you take it home to meet your mother?

Firstly, which direction does it face? North-facing is the most desirable aspect in the southern hemisphere because it'll give you the maximum amount of light. A westerly outlook will give you plenty of hot afternoon sun. Most plants need at least four–six hours of sunlight a day, so if your balcony gets less direct sun than that, you may have to contain your food garden in the sunniest section of your balcony, or use a sunny windowsill instead. There are some herbs and vegetables that will tolerate some shade, such as lettuce, mint, spinach or potatoes: your crop won't be as abundant but it will still give you a satisfying harvest. If your problem is too much hot sun, putting up a shadecloth might be the go.

If your balcony has an outside tap and a drain, you're cooking with gas. The tap will save you lugging a watering can back and forth from the kitchen, and a drain will ensure the water on your balcony runs off without drenching your neighbours below. (Try not to get neighbours offside over a garden. It's never worth it. Just ask France and Germany.)

If you don't have a drain there are a few solutions you can look at. Hydroponics, a system where plants grow in a container filled with a water-based nutrient solution rather than soil, is becoming more and more popular with home gardeners. The system only needs to be cleaned and flushed out once a year. (You can find more details at *abc.net.au/gardening/stories*.) If hydroponics sounds a little too high-tech for you, try raising your pots on a stand over a trough to catch the draining water. This water can then be re-used for the next watering.

Look at how exposed your balcony is. Many high-rise balconies are lashed by harsh winds. If this is the case with yours, you'll need to erect a windshield of sorts for your plants. This can be done by planting a hardy shrub or small tree in a pot, or by erecting some fencing material as a barrier. Breezes can be beneficial, as they keep plants aerated thus reducing fungal diseases, but strong winds can snap stems, 'burn' leaves and generally dehydrate your plants. If this is a regular problem for you, most edibles are going to really struggle: you may have to stick to low-growing herbs instead.

＊ The Aussie balcony is the great unsung hero of urban life.

Next, look at how sturdy your balcony is. What sort of weight could it take? You may have to check this with your building's body corporate if you're not sure. In many cases you'll need to minimise the extra weight you bring onto your balcony, which may affect your choice of planting system (the number and type of pots or containers you select, for example). Soil is also heavy so this needs to be factored into the equation, unless you go for a soil-free hydroponic system.

Finally, have a think about what climatic conditions prevail on your balcony. This is critical because it will affect the types of edibles you can grow and when you can grow them. Australia is roughly broken up into three growing regions: hot humid, hot dry and cool temperate (see the map below). Those of you lucky enough to live in the tropics will never see a true winter but will rather have to deal with hot and wet or hot and dry conditions. Warm-climate dwellers (like me in Sydney) will see more seasonal variation, with rain (or the lack of it) being the main issue. And those in the nippier parts of the country will get true seasons and will need to stick to their planting guides quite religiously.

Be aware that you may also have a microclimate at play. If your building is situated in a gully, on a ridge, near a creek or overlooking a busy road, these factors will all further affect your growing conditions. (If you do live on a busy road, be aware that the food you grow may absorb too many toxins from car exhaust fumes to be safely consumed, in which case you may want to reconsider growing outdoor food plants at all.)

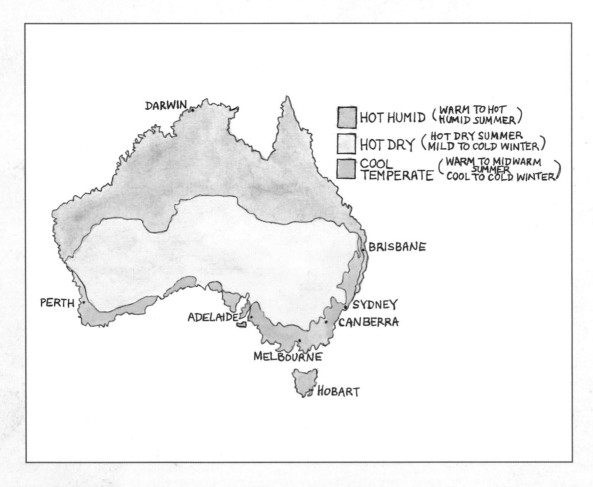

Going potty

I chose to plant in pots for three reasons. Firstly, I find pots are easier to move around the balcony if you need to isolate your plant from a pest infestation or the hot sun; secondly, pots require less technical know-how to master; and thirdly, the wide variety of pots available allows you to create a food garden with the shapes, colours and textures that reflect your personality.

Terracotta and concrete pots tend to be the heaviest, but there are lighter versions made from plastic, fibreglass or even sturdy fabric that you can use with excellent results (but keep in mind that plastic pots tend to trap heat). It may also be a good idea to invest in some pot stands with wheels to make any relocations easier on your back.

Select the right-sized pot for your plant. Too small and your plant won't have the room it needs to grow; too large and a small plant in the middle of a big pot will miss out on water, which tends to move to the extremities of a pot. Almost any vessel with some drainage holes (and some plastic lining if you're using an old basket, for instance) can be transformed into a planter. Whatever you use, good drainage is essential to prevent roots becoming waterlogged so don't let your plants sit in puddles or wet saucers. Keep your pots off the floor by using pottery feet, stands or even small bricks. And don't overcrowd your plants: give them plenty of room for air to circulate around them freely.

✳ Imagine that bleak concrete wall on your balcony as a veritable Hanging Gardens of Babylon.

Garden admin You'll soon discover that edible plants grow in all sorts of ways – up, down, across and over. Some will clump, others will sprawl, some will twist and climb and seem to want to reach for the stars. On a balcony, where space is an issue, many plants will need to be staked and trained to support their stems and fruit and to contain their spread. Take care when staking plants that you do not damage their delicate roots. Don't tie vines, stems or branches too tightly to your stakes: they will strangle the stems as the plants grow and cut off the food supply.

Don't forget that when your plant has finished cropping, the potting mix has been depleted of its nutrients and will need to be disposed of. Emptying pots will usually involve hauling your plants outside and spreading the contents on your apartment block's garden beds (ask permission first), or tipping the mix into your garden waste bin. Your pot then needs to be thoroughly scrubbed with a little bleach to ensure any bacteria from the previous crop doesn't infect your new planting. Skip your regular workout on these days! After emptying a few pots, you will huff and heave and sweat and possibly curse the day you ever dreamt of growing your own tomatoes.

Going up? Instead of, or as well as, using pots, you can explore the advances being made in vertical wall gardening. Once urban science-fiction, 'green wall' technology now has the potential to transform the way apartment-dwellers grow their food. Imagine that bleak concrete wall on your balcony as a veritable Hanging Gardens of Babylon.

You can start low-tech with a few hanging baskets and wall-mounted pots, or go the whole hog and install one of the seriously stylish, self-contained systems available (see page 141 for more information on the one I chose). These are ideal for busy urban professionals looking for a low-maintenance approach to food gardening. Most modern vertical wall systems will only support shallow-rooted herbs and lettuces, but that still leaves you with hundreds of edibles to choose from: try spinach, silverbeet and a host of Chinese greens such as tatsoi, pak choy and gai lan. Just remember to factor in your available sunlight and wind conditions.

Getting down to the nitty-gritty

The quality of the soil in which you plant your edibles will be the difference between sweet, flavoursome vegies and pale, limp imitations. Soil supplies your plants with virtually all the nutrients they need while they are growing, so it has to be top-class. Plants in containers require a special potting mix: soil from the garden just won't cut it. Potting mixes contain organic matter, compost, wetting agents and fertilisers that have been expertly blended to maximise the health of your plants. Good-quality organic potting mixes are readily available and cost around $18 for a 30-litre bag (never buy a potting mix for less than $5 for a 30-litre bag – you may as well be buying kitty litter). Generally it's cheaper to buy your potting mix than it is to make your own. Occasionally you may have a plant that has special soil requirements, such as a succulent or an orchid. I would recommend, however, that for growing edibles in

containers it is best to use a commercial potting mix (preferably an organic one), with a couple of handfuls of sand added to lighten your mix for better drainage. Just check that the potting mix carries the Australian Standard label on the pack.

Once opened, potting mixes dry out and begin to lose their potency, so it's important to buy only what you can use immediately, and don't leave them sitting around. Many quality potting mix brands now come in smaller 5-litre bags which are perfect for balcony gardeners. Be careful when working with potting mixes because they contain micro-organisms that may be hazardous to your health. The risk of contracting soil-borne diseases is negligible, although elderly gardeners can sometimes be vulnerable, so take precautions to be on the safe side. Always wear gloves when working with potting mix and wash your hands thoroughly afterwards. Never directly breathe the air of an opened potting-mix bag – use a dust mask for extra protection if you like.

Depending on the edibles you're growing, you may want to add some fertilisers to your potting mix to give the plants a nutrient boost. One size does not fit all, so do your research about what nutrients each plant prefers. Leafy greens, for example, like nitrogen-rich fertilisers, while other plants may like potassium or phosphorus as they're flowering or fruiting. You can find all of these additives at a good garden centre.

'Ow about a drink, love?

Pot plants are like front-bar regulars – they're thirsty drinkers. They lose moisture more rapidly than a plant in the ground and therefore need a good soak every few days, and every day in very hot weather. Watering your plants in this predominantly hot, dry country that is susceptible to prolonged droughts and subject to frequent water restrictions can be problematic, but these challenges are not insurmountable. Here are a few simple steps you can take to help limit your plants' water consumption.

- Select pots that retain moisture: terracotta pots may look attractive but because they are porous they tend to lose moisture at a faster rate than, say, a plastic container.

- Try to always water plants early in the morning or at night to reduce evaporation from the sun (or there are self-watering pots available that allow you to fill a reservoir at the base of the container and the plants' roots can draw up water as they need to).

- The general rule of thumb is the bigger the pot, the less water it will need, so try to stay clear of lots of little containers.

- Explore using mulches. These are ground covers made from organic material or pebbles that sit around the base of the plant, trapping moisture and dramatically reducing evaporation. Select a mulch that is suitable for your plant and low-maintenance: straw mulches may look rustic, but sweeping up bits of debris every time you have a wind gust will dull the romance somewhat.

If you have a balcony tap, you can attach a hose to it and water your plants directly. If not, you will need to use a watering can filled from indoors. However, if you plan to have a balcony garden larger than a few pots, I would recommend investing in an automatic drip irrigation system. These not only water your plants more efficiently, reducing wastage from spray and run-off, but ensure your plants are watered even when you're away (some food plants may never fully recover from the stress caused by a few instances of under-watering). Many edibles prefer to be watered at soil level rather than from overhead, so a drip system can potentially reduce any fungal and mould outbreaks your plants have to battle. Plastic irrigation piping and tubing systems are reasonably priced and available from most large hardware stores. You can cut the tubing to any length to fit the requirements of your potted garden – if I can install one with my limited Bob-the-Builder skills, I'm sure you can have a go. After you install a system, make sure you move the drippers around every week or so to stop water tracking along the same path and reducing your watering efficiency.

✳ Pot plants are like front-bar regulars – they're thirsty drinkers.

Of course, too much watering can be just as bad as not enough for some plants. A good way of testing whether a plant needs water is to poke part of your finger just below the soil surface. If it feels dry to the touch, it could do with a drink. If you have been neglectful in the watering department and find that water is running straight through your plants, it could be a sign that your potting mix has become hydrophobic, meaning water cannot stick to the soil particles. This can be easily corrected by immersing your pot in a bucket of water for 30 minutes or so to rehydrate the soil.

Watering is the most time-consuming weekly activity for a balcony food gardener. Once that's taken care of, you can spend more time enjoying the fruits of your labour.

Slugs, bugs and things that go chomp in the night

Also enjoying the fruits of your labour will be a host of pests. You'll develop a love/hate relationship with the insects that move into your balcony as soon as they spy your first green shoots. Since there aren't generally many plants in a built-up, urban environment, your edible balcony will become a Club Med of sorts to them, attracting all manner of sap-suckers, beetles and caterpillars keen to party.

Gardeners loosely classify insects into two categories – good bugs and bad bugs. The good bugs are basically the ones that assist you in your food-growing attempts: they pollinate the flowers on your herbs and vegetables, and eat the bad bugs. The bad bugs – well, they eat your plants. Particular plants will attract particular pests. Most predators tend to be active at night when they can carry out their food raids under the cover of darkness. Some caterpillars, laid as eggs by moths and butterflies on the underside of leaves, even burrow into the soil and emerge at dusk for their sorties. They are voracious feeders and just one can reduce a thriving mint patch to brown stems in hours – and reduce you to tears.

Getting the balance of good bugs and bad bugs right is an age-old frustration for gardeners. Usually it is achieved when a garden becomes its own healthy ecosystem; when everything is kept in check by everything else. Unfortunately, it can be difficult to develop a biodynamic balance on a small balcony with only four plants. The key is to know what attracts good bugs to your balcony, and what repels bad bugs. Some plants and flowers repel bad bugs with their odour. They can also mask the scent of tasty edibles, confusing those bad boys even further. For instance, tomatoes are said to repel flea beetles from cabbages, and marigolds not only provide a splash of colour but, when they're planted around your herbs and vegies, they can also fight off aphids and egg-laying moths.

Plants can be deployed to attract beneficial insects to your garden as well. The carrot, daisy and mint families are especially irresistible to good bugs; also try borage, calendula, lovage, yarrow and dill.

While the scientific community is yet to be fully convinced of these methods, generations of gardeners swear by them. From my limited experience, I think attractant and repellent plant pest control is worth exploring so you don't have to resort to using pesticides, which are not only harmful to you and your environment, but they will kill your good bugs as well.

✳ Most of your time should be spent not as a bad-bug pest-controller, but as a good-bug matchmaker.

Direct action There are a range of organic-certified sprays available that are safe to use, and you can even brew your own pest-control remedies. Try making a garlic spray to use on aphids, mealy bugs, white fly and mites. Finely mince 2 cloves garlic, add 2 teaspoons mineral oil (available from any hardware store), and leave for 24 hours. Then add 2 cups water and ½ tablespoon washing-up liquid. Stir well and strain into a jar to store. Add 1–2 tablespoons of this concentrate to 2 cups water and pour into a plastic spray bottle. Test a little on a leaf first and check in two days' time to make sure the spray has not affected the leaf, and then apply as

needed. Use sparingly as even garlic can kill good bugs if the concentration levels are too high.

You may be unlucky enough to find the odd brave slug or snail on your balcony (and if you are on the ground or lower floors, you may have plenty). These little blighters can be particularly difficult to control as they feed at night and hide during the day. They love to chomp on leaves, fruit and berries, and leave silvery trails of slime behind. They prefer moist, shady spots, so try tempting them out by placing some overturned citrus rinds near your affected plant, then collect the pests and destroy them (I squish mine). If they're still a problem, you could resort to a beer trap – bury a 5 cm-deep metal or plastic container so it is even with the soil surface. Half fill the container with beer and wait for the slugs and snails to fall in. Collect them in the early morning and destroy them before the sun drives them back into hiding.

Matchmaking Most of your time should be spent not as a bad-bug pest-controller, but as a good-bug matchmaker. Enlist your inner cupid to woo good bugs with bouquets and perfume. Planting attractant flowers, such as calendula and borage, around your edibles will keep the good bugs coming back to your balcony. Bees and hoverflies will be tempted to drop in and help pollinate your vegetable flowers, ladybirds will eat aphids and mealy bugs and help pollinate plants as well, green lacewings will devour a host of pests, spiders will trap insects in their webs and praying mantises will have a chomp at anything that moves.

Managing insects will be trial-and-error at first, but once you get the balance right it will greatly reduce your hours of pest patrol. And if you need a little outside intervention, there are even a few online pest-control companies that will send you some good predatory insects in the overnight mail! (See page 82 for more on this.) The best defence against pests is vigilance. Try to spend a few minutes every day inspecting your plants. Look on the underside of leaves for eggs, well-camouflaged caterpillars or aphid outbreaks. Look for tell-tale bite marks or shrivelled leaves. As with any good relationship, these quick daily inspections will ensure that potential problems are nipped in the bud.

How to become a seasoned performer

Understanding the effect the seasons will have on your edibles is critical to your success. The spring air will tease them out of their hibernation; the summer heat will accelerate their lush growth and intensify their flavours; the mellowness of autumn will mark an end for some and a new beginning for others; and root vegetables and leafy greens will relish the winter chill but pretty much everything else will hunker down and pull on their woollies. A reliable planting chart will become your botanical horoscope and you won't want to do anything without consulting it first, especially if you are considering purchasing seedlings. Some nurseries often sell plants out of season, which can be confusing for the novice: avoid buying these seedlings as they will struggle when you take them home and may fail to reach their full potential.

And remember that plants are classified as either annuals, biennials or perennials. Annuals die off after one year or one season, biennials complete their life cycle in two years (growing in the first year and flowering and fruiting in the second year), while perennials come back year after year. Broadly speaking, most vegetables are annuals, save for a few exceptions, and most herbs are perennials.

Doctor, I've got this rash . . .

It's not just insects that the balcony gardener will need to look out for. There are also a host of mildews, fungal diseases and blights that will rear their head every now and then, just when you think you can take a breather. They can be tackled with natural sprays and by ensuring you keep your plants healthy and robust: it's when your plants are weak or over-fertilised that the predators will strike. Here's a rundown of the main culprits:

DISEASE	APPEARANCE	TREATMENT
Blights	Leaves and branches suddenly wither, stop growing and die.	Remove and destroy affected areas. Use disease-free seed.
Galls	Galls are swollen masses of abnormal tissue. They can be caused by fungi, bacteria and certain insects. If you cut open a gall and there are no insects, you have a disease to deal with.	Prune away affected parts and disinfect tools with tea-tree oil to prevent contamination.
Mildews	Two main types – downy mildew and powdery mildew. Downy mildew appears as a white–purple downy growth on the undersides of leaves and along stems, which turns black with age. Powdery mildew attacks the upper surfaces of leaves and first appears as a white–greyish powdery growth.	For downy mildew: remove affected leaves and improve air circulation around plant by clearing away leaf matter. For powdery mildew: remove affected leaves immediately. Make a milk spray by mixing 1 part milk with 1 part tap water in a plastic spray bottle. At dusk, spray both sides of leaves. Avoid overhead irrigation.
Rots	Rots are diseases that decay roots, flowers and fruit. They can appear soft and spongy or hard and dry.	Remove and destroy affected plants.
Rusts	Rusts are a fungal disease. They appear as a powdery tan–rust-coloured coating.	Mulch, crop rotation. Avoid overhead irrigation.

Give plants the support they need

Sometimes, as we all know, the best support you can have is from a friend. There are some plants that are natural allies and support each other when grown in close physical proximity. This fascinating phenomenon is called companion planting and can spawn the most unlikely of friendships. For instance, carrots and onions thrive when planted next to each other, as they excrete chemicals into the soil that protect each other from pests and diseases. Some people believe basil is a good companion for tomatoes, repelling tomato whitefly. Conversely, some edibles need to be kept as far apart as Jennifer Aniston and Angelina Jolie. Cabbages and strawberries, for instance, should never attend the same awards-night ceremony. The table below lists the main edibles and their likes and dislikes.

PLANT	FRIEND	FOE
Beetroot	Bush bean, cabbage family, corn, leek, lettuce, lima bean, onion, radish.	Mustard, pole bean.
Broccoli	Beet, bush bean, carrot, celery, chard, cucumber, dill, kale, lettuce, mint, nasturtium, onion, oregano, potato, rosemary, sage, spinach, tomato.	Lima bean, pole bean, snap bean, strawberry.
Carrot	Bean, brussels sprouts, cabbage, chive, leaf lettuce, leek, onion, pea, pepper, red radish, rosemary, sage, tomato.	Celery, dill, parsnip.
Eggplant	Bush bean, pea, pepper, potato.	None.
Lettuce	Everything but especially carrot, garlic, onion and radish.	None.
Parsley	Asparagus, corn and tomato.	None.
Pea	Bean, carrot, celery, corn, cucumber, eggplant, parsley, radish, spinach, strawberry, sweet pepper.	Onion family.
Pepper	Carrot, eggplant, onion, parsnip, pea, tomato.	Fennel, kohlrabi.
Potato	Bush bean, cabbage family, eggplant, marigold, parsnip, pea.	Cucumber, pumpkin, raspberry, squash family, tomato, sunflower, turnip.
Pumpkin	Corn, eggplant, nasturtium, radish.	Potato.

PLANT	FRIEND	FOE
Radish	Bean, beet, cabbage family, carrot, chervil, cucumber, leaf lettuce, melon, nasturtium, parsnip, pea, spinach, squash family, sweet potato, tomato.	None.
Spinach	Cabbage family, celery, legumes, lettuce, onion, pea, radish, strawberry.	Potato.
Strawberry	Bean, borage, lettuce, onion, pea, spinach.	Cabbage family.
Tomato	Asparagus, basil, bush bean, cabbage family, carrot, celery, chive, cucumber, garlic, head lettuce, marigold, mint, onion, parsley, pepper, marigold.	Dill, fennel, pole bean, potato.

(adapted from *The Vegetable Gardener's Bible*, Edward C. Smith, Storey Publishing.)

Tools of the trade

Even on a small balcony you'll be surprised at the number of little maintenance jobs that will crop up from time to time, and you'll need to have the right equipment to make life a bit easier. Invest in a good pair of sturdy cotton gardening gloves to protect your hands from cuts, abrasions and soil bacteria. A small hand spade and fork will assist greatly when planting or re-potting. A pair of secateurs or garden scissors is useful for snipping off dead leaves and stems or harvesting fruit and sprigs of herbs. Twine and plant ties are also a must to secure delicate branches and emerging buds. Labelling your growing edibles is also a good idea, and there are many ways of doing this: I use cheap wooden craft sticks and a waterproof marker.

You'll also need an area in which to store your tools, spray bottles and fertilisers. Preferably this should be in a cool spot out of direct sunlight. My 'shed' is a large plastic storage box on wheels that slides away under my balcony bench. It's waterproof and large enough for me to be able to spot what I need without too much rummaging about.

Take care to disinfect garden tools before and after use when working with infected plants, so as not to spread disease.

ARE WE THERE YET?

Not quite, but almost. The actual planting and growing part of creating an edible balcony is a process that requires a little patience. Yes, patience – you know, that virtue we used to possess before iPhones and email reduced our attention span to that of a toddler's?

What was I saying? Oh yes . . . some things cannot be hurried, and food gardening is one of them. The rhythm of your life will begin falling back into step with the rhythm of nature. Twitter's need for constant input will exhaust you. Speed-dating will hold no allure and Twenty20 cricket will lose what limited appeal it had in the first place. You may even discover that Betty Crocker was never a real person, and attempt to whip up a cake from scratch.

You will learn that good things take time. A seed will sprout or a vegetable will ripen when it's good and ready, and not a second before. Waiting for this 'pay-off' is what modern pop psychology refers to as delayed gratification, which is often cited as the antidote to our hyper-frenetic lives. Well, delayed gratification is what edible gardening is all about. It's the languid, dark, smouldering Mr Darcy, when all you've known is the 'wham, bam, thank you ma'am' high-school stud.

We need a plan, Stan

The first thing you need to tackle is a planting map of your balcony. This doesn't have to meet the specifications of the *Architectural Digest*; all it needs to be is a quick hand-drawn sketch of your balcony's dimensions, showing where your pots and plantings will go (see my balcony plan for inspiration, opposite). When planning how much you can fit in the space you have, allow enough room for the size of your plants when they're fully grown, not the size they are when you put them in. This is a trap newcomers can easily fall into – Jiminy Cricket, I still do! Overcrowding will lead to spindly, weak plants and meagre harvests. And don't forget to make the most of your vertical space by using hanging baskets, shelving, wall-mounted containers and green-wall units (see page 141 for more on these). Some vegetables and fruits such as tomatoes, cucumbers and lemons can be trained on espaliers (trellises) to grow flat against a wall.

A plan will help you assess which vegetables you have room to grow and which are impractical wishful longings. Take into account the direction of your sunlight to make the best use of your space. And importantly, to maintain peace in your household, ensure your plan also accommodates your balcony's other uses. Leave room for relaxing, entertaining, drying clothes – and Fido's doggie bowls.

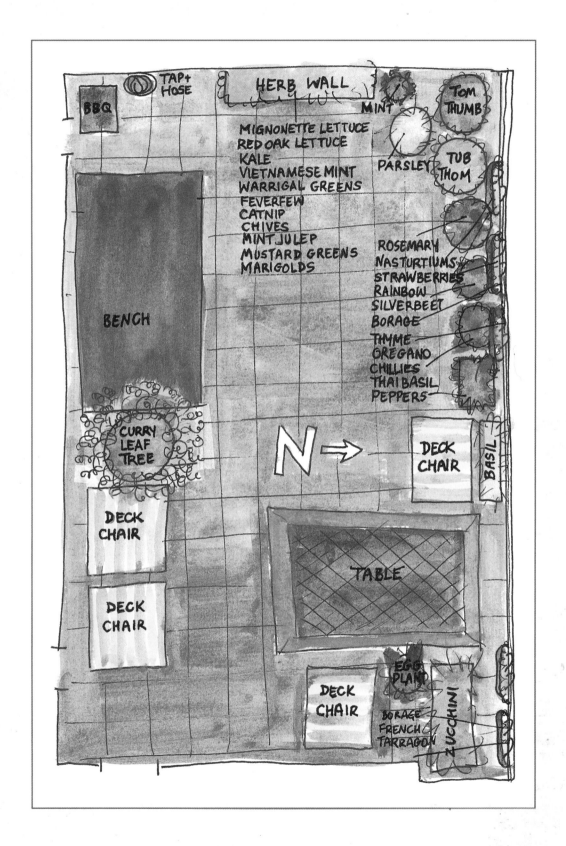

Planting the seed

Growing your herbs and vegetables from seed has two distinct advantages over nursery seedlings. Firstly, you will get a wider variety of stock to choose from, and secondly, seeds are far cheaper than seedlings. A packet of seeds will cost you between $2 and $5 and provide you with several seasons of vegetables. Depending on its maturity, a seedling will set you back anything from $4 to $25. And that's usually just for one plant that will usually die at the end of the season. If one of your main motivations for growing your own food is to save money, then seeds are definitely the better option.

Seeds are very precious parcels and require protection and safe-keeping until you're ready to plant them. They need to be kept in a cool, dry place where they can be easily identified. I fashioned a seed-storage container using an old gift box with some cardboard off-cuts as dividers. My seed packets are not organised alphabetically but filed under the calendar months they should be planted in, so I just flip through to September, for instance, and can immediately see what seeds I have to choose from for my spring plantings. Most seed packets come with helpful planting instructions. They'll recommend the best time of the year to grow your edibles, how much sunlight they require, how deep to bury them and how far apart they should be spaced. Heed their advice assiduously and many gardening calamities can be avoided.

Sowing seeds Most seeds can be sown directly into the container you've selected for them, although some may need to be sprouted indoors in a seed-raising mix and then planted outside when the weather warms up. Seed germinating trays for this purpose are available at most garden centres and nurseries. The best containers to use are ones that can be planted along with the seedling, reducing the risk of transplant damage to tender shoots. Select natural materials that will eventually break down in the soil, such as recycled egg cartons, eggshells, cardboard toilet-roll inners or small tubes made from a few layers of old newspaper. Be alert but not alarmed – even with diligent care, not all your seeds will germinate. Some have a use-by date; parsnip seeds, for instance, don't keep well after a year. This is why it's prudent to sow several seeds at a time to allow for the non-performers.

It's a jungle out there — searching for the right seed

There are dozens of seed companies and online seed distributors. My preferred suppliers are ones that sell non-hybrid, non-genetically modified seed that is chemical-free (see *diggers.com.au*, *thelostseed.com.au*, *fourseasonsherbs.com.au* and *theitaliangardener.com.au*). Many studies have shown that the plants from these seeds tend to grow true to type, are easier to grow, have significantly higher nutritional value, are more resistant to disease and pests, and produce over a longer season. Poring over seed catalogues and looking at the exotic range of heirloom varieties available will turn your notion of vegetables upside down. It will feel like opening a Dr Seuss book for the first time. You'll find seeds for purple carrots, candy-striped beetroot, yellow radishes, black peas and trombone-sized zucchinis. These heritage vegetables which have now all but disappeared from our supermarket shelves were once, before the widespread industrialisation of agriculture, popular and widely consumed. In many cases you'll also find they'll be tastier than their commercial counterparts and therefore require less preparation.

Seedlings — fast-track your vegies

If saving time rather than money is your priority, seedlings will certainly reduce some of that delayed gratification. Also, some herbs and vegetables such as lettuce are troublesome to grow from seed, and may require the professional skills of a nursery specialist to get them started. It's best to buy these as seedlings to save you some unnecessary angst. The widest range is available at garden centres and nurseries (steer clear of those consumptive specimens you see at the local supermarket). Select seedlings that are strong and healthy, and avoid any with yellow stems or leaves, or signs of pest or mould attack. A robust seedling will give you a sturdy, prolific plant. You'll need to re-pot your seedling into your chosen planter pot (see below).

Step 1 Fill the base of the pot with about 10 cm of gravel.

Step 2 Fill pot to three-quarters with potting mix and additives such as a little manure.

Step 3 Loosen the seedling from its pot and gently separate the bottom roots.

Step 4 Place the seedling in the pot and surround with potting mix until filled to just below the rim. Press the soil firmly around the base of the seedling and water well.

Making the first move — start simply with herbs

After absorbing these brief insights into what to plant and how to do it, you may have decided that a single pot of herbs is about all you can manage. This is totally fine. Don't let anyone make you feel like a piker.

Cultivating your own herbs will still give you that wonderful – and somewhat smug – satisfaction that comes from growing some of your own food. Balconies, terraces and courtyards are perfect spaces for growing herbs, as they thrive equally as well in pots as they do in garden beds. They require little maintenance and give a wonderfully intense, home-grown flavour to every meal they're added to. And the more you harvest them, the bushier and stronger they will grow. You'll also be surprised how much money you will save. A pot of basil or thyme or rosemary will turn into a money bush in no time at all. No more bunches of store-bought herbs wilting in plastic wrap in the fridge and then ending up as landfill. With a bunch costing anything between $2 and $5, the savings will quickly add up.

I know we all fear trying something new because we may fail. Food gardening is all about embracing this fear. There is a joy and sense of resilience we get from trying and failing, and trying and succeeding, that's exhilarating. I get such a buzz when I see my green pepper vine thriving on the balcony amidst the concrete, steel and tarmac.

It truly makes me feel that anything is possible.

The circle of life

Sometimes, despite every gardener's best efforts, things can go wrong, and plants will die for no apparent reason. It is often due to nothing more than a combination of inexperience, poor research and neglect. Try not to take these setbacks personally; we've all killed plants or had them die on us. It's upsetting and distressing and makes us feel like utter failures. It can be even harder to accept when a plant has been killed with kindness: excessive watering or too much fertiliser can be just as deadly as disregard.

I've found that understanding your plants' needs, rather than giving them what you think they need, is the first step to becoming a good food gardener. Plants have simple demands: they require sunlight, water, nutrients and a little shelter (they're similar to us in that way, really). Doing some research into what you're planting *before* you plant will save you plenty of angst, time and money in the long run. Sadly, it won't help save all your plants, but there will be the need for fewer burials.

Let the games begin

If I'd decided to stick to just growing a pot of herbs, I think my husband would have been a lot more relaxed about this whole edible balcony idea. Instead, he watched with increasing levels of anxiety as an assortment of large pots and sacks of potting mix and manure began to arrive, slowly encroaching on his precious outdoor space.

'It's a bombsite out there, Indira!' he said exasperatedly one morning, when he couldn't find room on the balcony to dry his towel.

'Yes, I'm *really* sorry about that,' I said, trying to defuse his rising temper. 'I want to see what herbs and vegetables will grow best on the balcony, so I've decided to road-test about forty different ones.' Seeing Mark's eyebrows shoot to the top of his hairline, I quickly rambled on, 'Don't worry, darling. Everything will be back to normal soon. You'll have the balcony back, I promise,' I said, hoping that would placate him. No chance.

'How soon is soon?' he asked slowly, scanning the mounds of muddy dirt and seed packets scattered across the tiles. A small vein was starting to pulsate on his damp brow.

'How does in about twelve months' time sound?' I said, feebly.

Life was about to get a whole lot more interesting . . .

RED OAK LETTUCE

BASIL

VIETNAMESE MINT

MINT

NASTURTIUM

CHIVES

MIGNONETTE LE

RED HORN PEPP

BUTTER LETTUCE

TUB TOM TOMAT

ZUCCHINI

ZUCCHINI FLOU

CHERRY TOM

SUMMER

There's nothing quite like summer on the edible balcony. The days are filled with the hypnotic hum of cicadas, smoky aromas from outdoor barbecues, tangy gusts of hot sea air and the floral perfume of the season's first vine-ripened tomatoes. Bring it on!

IN THE BEGINNING

In this sub-tropical heat the balcony is slowly transforming. Where once there were only concrete and cold tiles, now there are sprouts and seedlings squirming into life. The pots are bursting with buds and shoots: the hint of tiny flowers yet to emerge. I'm delightfully amazed. Things are actually growing! My keenly awaited summer crop will include tomatoes, basil, eggplant, red horn peppers, zucchini, lettuce, mint, chives and nasturtium flowers. A little ambitious, perhaps?

Like many relationships forged in the heat of passion, my edible balcony is now gradually evolving into an all-consuming obsession. It's the first thing I think about when I wake up in the morning, and the last thought I have as I drift off to sleep. My bedside table is piled high with gardening bibles and yellowed, dog-eared finds from second-hand bookshops. To my bemused friends and family, I am becoming that slightly odd woman who used to have a 'firm grip on things'.

Doubt still gnaws at my tentative confidence though. I monitor my plants the way a new mother constantly checks her baby for signs of breathing. As soon as I'm awake, I'm up and out on the balcony, anxiously inspecting every leaf, every blossom for bugs or disease. I'm still not wholly sure what I'm supposed to be looking for. My plants' main health risk could quite possibly be from my over-attentiveness. I definitely need to relax a little. Let's face it, in the grand scheme of things, growing vegetables is easy compared to, say, trying to stop Kyle Sandilands from offending someone.

> ✳ Like many relationships forged in the heat of passion, my edible balcony is now gradually evolving into an all-consuming obsession.

YOU SAY 'TOMAYTO', I SAY 'TOMAHTO' . . .

Tomatoes are often the first vegetable new gardeners will tackle successfully; they're relatively easy to grow and produce prolific quantities of fruit. You may be unlucky enough to get a white fly attack or an aptly named blight, but generally speaking, growing tomatoes is pretty straightforward.

In November I took advantage of a week of warm weather and planted two seedlings, a heritage cherry variety and a slightly larger Tub Tom. It was Melbourne Cup week, and I must have been the only Aussie who didn't stop for the race. Instead, I was elbow-deep in manure and mud (actually, come to think of it, it *was* a lot like being at the Melbourne Cup . . .).

Getting my seedlings in early in the season certainly seemed to help. I used an organic potting mix, some slightly pongy sheep manure and a little blood and bone to give them a nutrient boost. As the vines grew, I pinched out the side shoots so that all the plant's energy went into fruit production. I used plastic ties and wooden stakes to support the delicate vines as they fanned out like arteries. By early December, the bushes were lush with foliage and had hundreds of tiny, star-like yellow flowers.

It seemed my earlier unease was unfounded. There were soon tomatoes, and lots of them. These two bushes eventually produced about 10 kilos of fruit over the summer. Until you've picked a home-grown tomato you cannot imagine how good they can smell; sweet and fragrant, occasionally with just a hint of Turkish delight. Where does that aroma come from, I wonder? Even the leaves smell good. How hedonistic to eat pesticide-free tomatoes straight off the vine: no washing under the tap, just a quick wipe on your sleeve then straight into your mouth. Juicy and sweet, with a faint balancing note of bitterness. Nothing like the mealy, pink-ish impersonators you'll find in the supermarkets. Now I know why Eve couldn't resist that apple, because apparently it was more likely to have been a tomato, since apples don't grow in Middle Eastern climates.

Tomatoes

When to plant? Hot humid climate Year-round Hot dry climate August–December Cool temperate climate September–November

Seed or seedling? Seedling.

I like . . . full sun and free-draining soil. Some varieties need to be staked.

I don't like . . . frosts; pests such as fruit fly, aphids, caterpillars and tomato russet mites.

Feed me . . . liquid fertiliser every two weeks.

Give me a drink . . . regularly: don't let soil dry out or fruit will lose its sweetness.

Pick me . . . just before fruit is ripe. Ripen fruit indoors in a dark place.

Tomato, butter bean and chorizo salad

If only travelling was as easy as daydreaming about it. That's when food can be a close substitute. This salad is very similar to one I had at a tapas bar at the La Boqueria Market in Barcelona. Use the best chorizo you can find for a delicious whack of smoky paprika.

Serves 4 as a side dish or 2 as a main course

100–150 g canned butter or cannellini beans, thoroughly washed and drained

20 cherry tomatoes, halved

½ red onion, thinly sliced

handful flat-leaf parsley leaves, roughly chopped

olive oil, for pan-frying

250 g mild or spicy chorizo, diced

salt and freshly ground black pepper

Sherry vinegar dressing

1 clove organic garlic, crushed

1 tablespoon sherry vinegar or red-wine vinegar

squeeze of lemon (optional)

⅓ cup (80 ml) extra virgin olive oil

salt and freshly ground black pepper

- Place the beans, tomatoes, onion and parsley in a bowl.
- To make the dressing, place all the ingredients in a jar with a screw-top lid and shake to combine. Pour the dressing over the salad and set aside for 5–10 minutes for the flavours to infuse.
- Meanwhile, heat a frying pan over medium–high heat and add the oil to the pan. Toss in the chorizo and cook for a minute or two until crispy.
- To serve, arrange the salad on a plate, scatter the chorizo on top and serve immediately.

Homemade tagliatelle with cherry tomatoes, basil, garlic and chilli

Serves 4

⅓ cup (80 ml) extra virgin olive oil

5 cloves organic garlic, thinly sliced

2 cups (320 g) cherry or grape tomatoes

½ teaspoon dried chilli flakes

2 handfuls basil leaves

salt and freshly ground black pepper

½ cup (40 g) parmesan

Tagliatelle

2 cups (300 g) '00' bread flour, plus extra for dusting

3 organic eggs

pinch of salt

I always thought that making my own pasta wouldn't be worth the effort. After all, how could going to the trouble of making a fresh pasta dough, kneading it, resting it and then running it through a pasta machine possibly give you a better result than the no-fuss, shop-bought variety?

How very wrong I was. Freshly made egg pasta is one of life's true pleasures; silky-smooth, comforting and highly addictive. And the more often you use your hand-cranked pasta machine, the more proficient you'll get and the better the results will be. Go on – channel your inner Nonna.

- To make the tagliatelle, sift the flour onto a clean benchtop. Make a well in the centre, then add the eggs and salt. Work the mixture until it comes together, gradually incorporating all of the flour. Wash your hands, then knead the dough for 10–15 minutes until it is smooth and elastic. Cover with plastic film and leave to rest for 30 minutes.

- Cut the dough into five or six pieces. Dusting well with flour as you go, put each piece through a pasta machine, starting at the widest setting and moving through to the narrowest until you have a translucent sheet to put through the tagliatelle cutter. Drape the tagliatelle over a suspended wooden spoon or broom handle to dry for 5–10 minutes before cooking.

- To make the sauce, heat 3 tablespoons oil in a large frying pan over low heat and cook the garlic for 5 minutes or until soft but not coloured. Add the tomatoes and increase the heat to medium–high. Throw in the chilli and half the basil leaves, season to taste and cook for 8–10 minutes until tomatoes have collapsed.

- Cook the pasta in a large saucepan of boiling salted water for about 4 minutes or until al dente. Keep an eye on it – you don't want to overcook it and waste all that hard work!

- As soon as the pasta is cooked, drain and add to the tomato sauce. Don't rinse it as this will wash off the starchy water that will help thicken your sauce. Turn the heat off, add the grated cheese, drizzle over the remaining olive oil and stir well. Top with the remaining basil leaves and serve.

Gazpacho oyster shooters

These shooters are decadent and refreshing. I think our indigenous Sydney rock oysters are some of the best oysters in the world: for their tiny size they pack a briny punch that is unrivalled. Of course, you can use whatever oyster variety you find at your local fish markets. Just make sure they're squeakily fresh. If you want to give these shooters an extra pick-me-up, add a dash of vodka to each one.

Makes 12

3 cloves organic garlic

salt and freshly ground black pepper

1 kg ripe tomatoes, halved

1 green capsicum (pepper), seeds and white membrane removed, flesh sliced

1 small Lebanese cucumber, peeled, seeded and chopped

½ small brown onion, finely grated

¼ cup chopped coriander leaves, plus stalks to garnish

2 cups (140 g) coarse breadcrumbs, made from day-old bread

3 tablespoons good-quality red-wine vinegar

⅓ cup (80 ml) extra virgin olive oil

12 freshly shucked oysters

- Crush the garlic to a paste in a mortar and pestle with a good pinch of salt.

- Place the tomato, capsicum, cucumber, onion, coriander and coarse breadcrumbs in a food processor and puree until smooth (or you can do this with a stick blender). Pass the mixture through a sieve to give a fine texture. Stir in the garlic paste, vinegar and oil and season to taste with salt and pepper. Cover and place in the fridge to chill for 2 hours.

- To serve, place an oyster at the bottom of 12 shot glasses, top with the gazpacho and garnish with a coriander stalk.

Tomato kasundi

This is a very popular sauce from the Gujarat region of India. It goes wonderfully with finger foods: try it with the Stuffed Zucchini Flowers on page 60, or the Potato, Pea and Coriander Samosas on page 119.

Makes 1 cup

5 large ripe tomatoes

1 tablespoon vegetable oil

2 cloves organic garlic, sliced

½ teaspoon mustard seeds

1 teaspoon cumin seeds

1 teaspoon coriander seeds

½ teaspoon ground turmeric

1 teaspoon cayenne pepper

½ teaspoon salt

¼ cup white vinegar

1 preserving jar, sterilised (see page 65)

- First, blanch the tomatoes to make them easier to peel. With a sharp knife score the top of the tomatoes with a small cross, being careful not to cut too deep. Bring a large saucepan of water to the boil, carefully place the tomatoes in and remove the pan from the heat. Leave for about 30 seconds then remove the tomatoes with a slotted spoon and place in a colander. Peel each tomato and discard the skin, then chop the flesh roughly.

- Heat the oil in a large heavy-based saucepan over low–medium heat. Add the garlic and mustard seeds and stir for 1–2 minutes until the seeds start to pop. Turn the heat up to medium–high and add the cumin and coriander seeds, the turmeric, cayenne pepper, salt and tomatoes. Cook, stirring, for 5 minutes. Add the vinegar and bring to the boil, then reduce the heat, cover and simmer for 15 minutes until the sauce thickens.

- Spoon into the prepared jar and seal. Once opened, the kasundi will keep in the fridge for 2–3 weeks.

ABANDONING MY BABIES

It looked as though we were in for a hot summer; it was only early December and the mercury was already creeping into the 30s. Not the best time to leave the plants and go overseas for three weeks. Why hadn't I put a drip irrigation system in earlier?

'Do you think we could take some of the plants with us?' I asked Mark one evening, only half in jest, as we were planning our schedule.

'What do *you* think?' Mark said, having long since lost his sense of humour where the plants were concerned.

'Okay,' I continued, 'but we're going to have to ask a friend to stay over while we're away to water them.'

'That's ridiculous!' he shot back. 'A house-sitter just for some plants? Who's going to do that? Why don't we just ask the building concierge to look after them and give him a bottle of bubbly for his trouble?'. His solution sounded far too reasonable. I had to disagree.

'But we don't know if he'll have enough time to water the plants regularly, or, or . . . whether he knows anything *about* plants!' I said.

'He's a country bloke. He grew up around trees. He'll be fine,' said Mark.

I couldn't recall ever seeing any of my inner-city friends using a watering can so Darrell the concierge was probably going to be my best bet.

So, with my tomato bushes dense with fruit and the other summer herbs and vegetables just kicking into life, I bid my plants a guilty farewell, certain I would return to an edible graveyard. Of course, their wellbeing haunted me throughout the trip. From San Francisco to Washington to New York, I constantly checked the Sydney weather forecast online, fearing heatwaves or violent summer storms. I even considered ringing Darrell for an update.

There was no sympathy from Mark. He said my CPSA – Chronic Plant Separation Anxiety – was becoming really annoying. In fact, why were we having this conversation, he said, when we should be taking in the Manhattan skyline? I guess I was being ridiculous fretting over a few vegetables I began growing, ironically, to help me *relax*. Of course the plants were being well-looked after. Darrell was Mr Reliable. He wouldn't let anything happen to them. I tucked my scarf firmly under my chin, pulled my beanie down securely and hurried after Mark along the icy Brooklyn foreshore. Mark knew that food, and lots of it, was always a good way of distracting me. After a lunch appetiser of Margherita pizza cooked in a coal-fired brick oven at Brooklyn's legendary Grimaldi's pizzeria, followed by a lobster tasting plate at The River Café nearby, I soon forgot I even *had* a balcony.

THE AFTERMATH

You know those home makeover shows when Jamie or Scott or Johanna bring in an excited family and unveil their new garden? Well, when we returned to Sydney and I walked out onto my balcony for the first time, I was expecting a balcony blitzkrieg. How could any of my plants have survived in my absence? I was steeling myself for shrivelled fruit, emaciated stalks and desiccated foliage. It would be plant carnage.

Instead, what greeted me was far more emotionally confronting. There was no carnage; instead, the balcony had morphed into an unbelievably green, lush oasis. The plants had all tripled in size! Everywhere I looked there were bushes abundant with leaves, flowers and fruit. They had clearly thrived under Darrell's care. In fact, they seemed to have responded to him a little *too* well for my liking – the only immediate maintenance they needed was a little pruning back. I was suddenly a whirl of neuroses. As I inspected each healthy plant my insecurity deepened. What had Darrell given them that I couldn't provide? Had my babies found a new mommy?

I went downstairs to thank Darrell for his wonderful efforts and to secretly pump him for information. What had he done that had made the plants respond so well? Nothing, he said. How often had he watered them? Just followed your instructions, he said. Did he do anything unusual, such as talking to them or playing them music? No, he said, somewhat taken aback. What then, I asked exasperatedly? I could see my interrogation was beginning to make Darrell a little uncomfortable. He suggested that maybe it was because he had been fairly relaxed about it. Was he implying that I *wasn't* relaxed? Was he? No, that's not what he was saying at all, he assured me, although if this conversation continued along these lines he was going to have to reassess his opinion. He was right. I apologised to Darrell for my unreasonably harsh cross-examination, putting it down to jet-lag.

Back upstairs on the balcony I slumped into a deckchair and quietly surveyed the garden. It wasn't jet-lag. I was plagued with self-doubt. Of course I was happy the plants had been well-looked after in my absence – I would have been devastated if anything had happened to them. But if learning to relax a bit more was going to make me a better gardener, then that's what I was determined to try to do from now on. 'Aummm,' I hummed, while attempting to fold my legs into the lotus position.

YOU PUT BASIL IN THE RATATOUILLE?

Is there anything more erotic than basil? I find its aniseed-flavoured leaves, whether fresh, crushed or wilted, a pure aphrodisiac. Just brushing past a basil bush will release its volatile minty oils. There are more than ten varieties of this versatile herb available, from lemon and cinnamon-flavoured to Greek and Thai. The most popular variety is common sweet basil, which produces large billowing leaves that make a delicious pesto.

Basil is well suited to a balcony garden: it is very low-maintenance and a prolific grower.

It is regarded as a good companion plant for tomatoes, so I planted two common sweet basil seedlings with each tomato plant. (The basil is a white-fly deterrent for the tomatoes and seems to impart some of its complementary aniseed flavours as well.) You'll need a good-sized pot to accommodate the basil's large root ball, and be careful not to crowd the seedlings, leaving at least 20 cm between each plant. Plant in with some organic soil and manure.

With plenty of sunlight and water, the basil grew to almost a metre high. I pinched off the top leaves regularly to encourage thicker growth. You may also need to apply an occasional squirt of a petroleum-based spray oil (or 'pest oil') if aphids attack. This kills the aphids but won't affect your plants, and can be bought from nurseries, garden centres and even some supermarkets.

Basil

When to plant? Hot humid climate Year-round Hot dry climate August–March
Cool temperate climate September–February

Seed or seedling? Either.

I like . . . the heat; a sunny well-drained area.

I don't like . . . the cold; slugs and snails.

Feed me . . . liquid fertiliser every month.

Give me a drink . . . once or twice a week, and more regularly in summer.

Pick me . . . as needed. Pinch off flowers to encourage bushy leaves.

Basil pesto

It's a little known (and slightly bizarre) fact that in 2004 I was sworn in as a member of the Order of the Knights of the Pesto Brotherhood while on assignment for *Australian Gourmet Traveller* in Genoa, Italy. The Pesto Brotherhood is an organisation that is committed to the protection of authentic pesto sauce which it believes can only be called pesto if it is made using the local basil leaves grown in Genoa. I have to agree with the Brotherhood that the best pesto I've tasted was made using Genovese basil. It has a very intense aniseed–minty flavour. While you can't get Genovese basil in Australia, the common sweet basil that I grow is a pretty good substitute.

There's always a jar of fresh pesto in our fridge. We like to spread it on toast, spoon it over hot pasta or stir it through a minestrone soup.

Makes 1 cup

2 firmly packed cups (160 g) basil leaves

1 clove organic garlic, peeled

⅓ cup (50 g) pine nuts

3 tablespoons grated parmesan

½ cup (125 ml) extra virgin olive oil, plus extra to cover

salt and freshly ground black pepper

- Put the basil, garlic and pine nuts in a mortar and pestle or small food processor and grind until a rough paste forms. Stir in the cheese. Slowly pour in a thin stream of oil and stir until you reach the desired consistency. Taste and season with salt and pepper.

- Spoon into an airtight container, cover with a thin layer of olive oil, and store in the fridge for up to 2 weeks.

Pizza Margherita

Makes 2

1 cup (280 g) tomato pasta sauce

8 ripe tomatoes, sliced

200 g buffalo mozzarella, sliced

⅓ cup Basil Pesto (see page 47)

2 handfuls basil leaves

nasturtium flowers, to garnish (optional)

Pizza dough

4 cups (600 g) plain flour

pinch of salt

1 × 7 g sachet dried yeast

½ teaspoon sugar

1¾ cups (435 ml) warm water

1 tablespoon olive oil

Despite being born in South Africa to Indian parents, and raised in England, Zimbabwe and Australia, Italy is where my foodie heart actually yearns to be; its rich, volcanic soils turn out the most extraordinary tasting produce. You haven't tasted a tomato until you've tasted one grown under the Mediterranean sun along the southern coastline of Campania.

My home-grown balcony tomatoes are the next best thing. Their sweetness really shines when combined with fresh basil leaves and buffalo mozzarella in this classic pizza combo.

- To make the pizza dough, sift the flour and salt into a bowl and stir in the yeast and sugar. Combine the warm water and oil in a jug then pour into the dry ingredients and mix with a flat-bladed knife until the mixture just comes together. Tip out onto a clean benchtop and knead for 10 minutes until smooth and elastic. Place the dough in an oiled bowl and cover with plastic film and a tea towel. Set aside in a warm place for 30 minutes or until doubled in size.

- Preheat fan-forced oven to 250°C. Lightly oil two baking trays and place in the oven to warm.

- When the dough has risen, knock out the air with your fist and divide into two portions. Roll out each portion into a large rectangle and place on a hot baking tray. Spread with tomato sauce and sliced tomato, then top with mozzarella and bake for 15–20 minutes or until the cheese has melted and the crust sounds hollow when tapped.

- Remove from the oven and scatter over a few dollops of pesto, some whole basil leaves and nasturtiums, if using.

Basil ice cream

After competing in the dessert challenge in *Celebrity MasterChef*, I vowed to master my ice-cream-making technique (being shamed on national television is a great motivator). I promptly bought an ice-cream machine and did lots of research on what makes a fabulous-tasting ice cream.

This recipe, adapted from one I came across in *delicious*. magazine, calls for the unusual combination of fresh basil leaves and yoghurt, and it's a perfect palate-cleansing dessert to have after a spicy meal. Many ice creams can be made by hand, but for this one you'll need an ice-cream machine.

Makes 1.8 litres

3 large handfuls basil leaves, washed and dried well, plus extra to garnish

400 g caster sugar

250 g light cream cheese, softened

1 kg thick Greek-style yoghurt

- Place the basil leaves and sugar in a food processor and blend to a coarse powder. Add the cream cheese and yoghurt then pulse to combine.

- Churn the mixture in an ice-cream machine according to the manufacturer's instructions, then freeze until firm (about 4–5 hours).

- Serve garnished with the extra basil leaves.

THE DAYS GROW HOTTER AND WETTER

Over Christmas and the New Year, the edible balcony became an outdoor entertainment larder of sorts. It was frequently raided of its mint for cocktails, chives for hors d'oeuvres, and basil and tomatoes for hastily thrown-together pizzas. The hungry partying hordes left very happy. Life on the balcony was going well, too well. I should have seen it coming. In early February, the Revenge of the Caterpillars began.

The attacks started quietly enough, with a few frayed leaves the only sign that something was amiss. The operatives were well camouflaged. But as more and more leaves on the tomato, pepper, mint and basil plants started resembling green doilies, I went in for a closer inspection. I found that the undersides of the leaves were dense with bright green caterpillars, where earlier visiting moths and butterflies had cunningly laid their eggs. I soon realised that detecting these little chomping accordions was only half the battle. They attached themselves

to the leaves with their huge anchor-like teeth, and put up quite a struggle against my forceful tugs. Extricating them without crushing them in a spurt of green ooze was tricky; they were determined little buggers. I could see now why so many gardeners turned to pesticides. Hand-picking those bugs off the leaves was time-consuming and messy, and organic sprays didn't seem to work fast enough. And just when I thought I'd got them all, the next morning another leaf would start to disappear, sending me into a spiral of angry frustration.

Being bigger, and meaner, and only slightly smarter than the bugs had its advantages though. I learnt to follow their tiny black poo trails back to the source. I called this the Hansel and Gretel pest-control method. Then the assaults ended, as suddenly as they had begun. Exhausted, I surveyed the damage. Most of the edibles had somehow survived with only a few war-wounds. While many leaves had been devoured, the flowers and the all-important fruit buds had remarkably remained intact. I, on the other hand, needed a very long drink. Actually, could you make that a double? (Here's my recipe for Caterpillar Recovery Tonic: half-fill a shot glass with butterscotch schnapps and top up with kahlua. Keep refilling until the pain subsides.)

LETTUCE BE

Lettuce is a meal in itself. To me, a simple wedge of iceberg lettuce with a drizzle of mayonnaise vinaigrette is five-star dining at home. It can also give welcome texture to an array of meals, such as a crunchy noodle salad, coleslaw or a stir-fry. No edible balcony is complete without a tub of lettuce.

Lettuce gets my *Vegetable Gardening for Dummies* award. If you can boil water, you can grow lettuce. It's the partner we all wished we had – low-maintenance with no hang-ups. Lettuce comes in dozens of varieties: there's rocket, mignonette, butter, coral, iceberg, radicchio, mustard greens, mizuna, watercress . . . the list goes on. From wondrous shades of green to deep red, from sweet to peppery to bitter, there's really something for everyone. I planted a mix of mignonette, butter lettuce, rocket, watercress and some mustard greens in late summer when the weather was just cooling (lettuces will go limp in the heat).

Lettuces are shallow-rooted so will grow very well in containers: I planted mine in some 20 cm-deep baskets attached to my balcony railing. They need a lot of water and their biggest enemies are grubs and strong direct sun. In warm weather, keep your crop in a shady corner of your balcony or under a shadecloth, douse them with some seaweed fertiliser every two weeks or so and you will have an almost continuous supply of fresh, crunchy leaves. Pick the outer leaves first so the new juicy inner leaves can sprout. Unlike most veggies, lettuces benefit from the occasional overhead watering as they can absorb nutrients through their leaves as well as their roots. I had to battle a few aphid attacks and some white-fly incursions on my lettuces, but overall they thrived, especially when the temperatures dipped in late February and early March.

Butter, mignonette and red oak lettuces

When to plant? Hot humid climate Year-round Hot dry climate Year-round Cool temperate climate Year-round

Seed or seedling? Seedlings are easier.

I like . . . a sunny position in rich, well-draining soil.

I don't like . . . the summer heat (some varieties can bolt); slugs and snails.

Feed me . . . fortnightly liquid fertiliser feeds will bring on rapid growth.

Give me a drink . . . often, and every day in the heat of summer.

Pick me . . . as required; pick outer leaves only.

Pork sang choy bau

Makes 10

1 tablespoon vegetable oil

1 tablespoon sesame oil

2 cloves organic garlic, crushed

2 tablespoons grated ginger

4 spring onions, green and white parts finely chopped

500 g minced pork

100 g water chestnuts, drained and finely chopped

3 tablespoons oyster sauce, plus extra to serve

2 tablespoons soy sauce

3 tablespoons Chinese shaohsing rice wine

1 tablespoon sugar

10 butter lettuce leaves, washed, trimmed and kept in iced water

black or white sesame seeds, toasted

chopped chive stems, to garnish

Butter or iceberg lettuce leaves make perfect sturdy containers for holding fillings. This dish is a particular favourite with kids because they can spoon in their own filling and use their hands to fold the leaves into bite-sized parcels. Adults enjoy them too! Cool and crisp on the outside; warm and exotic on the inside.

If you can't find black sesame seeds, which impart a slightly bitter flavour to this dish, white sesame seeds will do just fine. Toast them first to enhance their nutty flavour. You can substitute sherry for the shaohsing rice wine but you won't get the same complex flavour.

- Heat the vegetable and sesame oils in a large frying pan over medium heat. Add the garlic, ginger and finely chopped white part of the spring onions and cook for 5 minutes, stirring frequently so the mixture doesn't catch and burn. Add the minced pork and stir-fry for 3–4 minutes. Stir in the water chestnuts, oyster sauce, soy sauce, rice wine and sugar. Taste and adjust the seasoning if necessary to ensure there is a nice salty–sweet balance. Simmer for 5 minutes or until the liquid has reduced to a thick and syrupy consistency. Remove from the heat and stir in the green part of the spring onions.

- Drain the lettuce leaves and wipe gently with paper towel to remove all water.

- Fill each lettuce cup with the pork mixture, finishing with a dollop of oyster sauce and a sprinkling of black or white sesame seeds, and garnish with a chive stem.

Mignonette and red oak lettuce with gruyere, Dijon vinaigrette and garlic croutons

I adore wandering through food markets on my travels. One of my favourites is the Union Square Greenmarket in New York City, where farmers sell more than a thousand different varieties of fresh produce. Tucked away just behind the square on East 16th Street is The Union Square Cafe, which transforms market produce into simple seasonal dishes. They serve a salad similar to this one.

Serves 4 as an entree

1 small clove organic garlic

2 tablespoons olive oil

4 slices sourdough bread, crusts removed

2 tablespoons red-wine vinegar

1 teaspoon Dijon mustard

3 tablespoons extra virgin olive oil

salt and freshly ground black pepper

3 tablespoons grated gruyere, plus extra to serve

4 handfuls mixed mignonette and red oak lettuce leaves, trimmed and washed

marigold petals, to garnish

- Preheat fan-forced oven to 180°C.

- Pound the garlic using a mortar and pestle until a paste forms. Stir in the oil and brush this mixture over the bread slices. Cut the bread into cubes, then spread out on a baking tray and bake for 10 minutes or until crunchy and slightly golden. Remove from the oven and drain on paper towel.

- Whisk together the vinegar, mustard, extra virgin olive oil, salt and pepper in a large bowl until well incorporated. Stir in the cheese.

- Toss the lettuce lightly in the dressing and arrange on a serving plate. Drizzle some of the dressing over the top, then scatter over the croutons, a little extra cheese and some marigold petals to serve.

BLOOMING MARVELLOUS

Am I the only gardener who grows zucchinis for their flowers, not their fruit? I hope not. Whoever discovered that these large, velvety flowers were edible hit upon a taste bonanza. Those soft egg-yellow petals that open into a golden chalice are just made for stuffing with exotic fillings. Zucchini flowers stuffed with cheese, crumbed and shallow-fried would quite simply be my death-row meal, although only Matt Preston could eat at a time like that.

For the impatient gardener, zucchini plants may be just the thing. They are fast-growing and produce prolific quantities of fruit. The downside is that they can ramble if left unchecked. They will take over your little container vegetable patch in no time with their long, finely spiked stalks and broad leaves. They will steal the light from other plants and stealthily encroach on their space. They are not always a welcome tenant.

I planted three seeds in early February, two pale green Lebanese varieties and one of the more common Blackjacks. I soon realised that one seed would have sufficed. In four weeks, all three bushes were already a metre high and 2 metres wide. They soon blocked the light from the eastern corner of the balcony. Mark began walking around with his 'Not happy, Jan!' face on – this was the triffid-like scenario he had dreaded. Thankfully he did a bit of grunting, but said nothing.

Six weeks after planting, the first zucchini flowers appeared. The flowers come in male and female form: the male flowers sit on long thin stalks while the female flowers are attached to miniature zucchinis. The flowers were like folded golden parasols with pale green, tapering spines and puckered lips. Too beautiful to eat.

Almost.

ZUCCHINI IVF

Some vegetables, such as tomatoes and capsicums, self-pollinate but others, such as zucchinis, need outside intervention. If you don't have many insects around to help you pollinate your flowers, you may be required to assist with a little matchmaking. When the male and female flowers have opened, take a soft clean paintbrush and lightly tap it against the stamen in the male flower until the bristles are covered with yellow powdery pollen. Be gentle. You don't want to break the delicate stamens. Now tap the brush very gently onto the stigma sitting in the centre of the female flower and wait for the magic to begin.

I left two female flowers to develop into full-sized fruit; the rest would be stuffed. Harvesting the flowers was trickier than I realised. Flowers that are already open are easier to prepare and I discovered that each fragile bloom opened once at sunrise, and then only for a few hours before it closed and wilted. So, at the crack of dawn one morning, armed with my secateurs, I went in for the big cull. The flowers were pointed at the morning sun like big orange satellite dishes. I thought I heard a soft sigh each time I snipped, but this wasn't possible, was it? Plants don't make any noise, or do they? It was unsettling.

The sound I did enjoy hearing, though, was the crumbed flowers sizzling in a pan of hot olive oil. All was right with the world again.

Zucchinis and zucchini flowers

When to plant? Hot humid climate January–March, August–December
Hot dry climate September–December Cool temperate climate October–December

Seed or seedling? Seed.

I like . . . full sun and well-draining soil.

I don't like . . . roots getting waterlogged, or they can develop mildew.

Feed me . . . once a fortnight with fertiliser until flowers form.

Give me a drink . . . regularly, particularly in warm weather.

Pick me . . . from six weeks, flowers can be harvested or left to develop into zucchinis.

Stuffed zucchini flowers

Serves 3–4 as an entree

250 g fresh full-fat ricotta

3 tablespoons
grated parmesan

1 tablespoon rinsed
and drained capers,
roughly chopped

1 tablespoon chopped basil

freshly ground black pepper

6 zucchini (courgette)
flowers with the tiny
zucchini attached

⅔ cup (100 g)
self-raising flour

2 organic eggs,
lightly beaten

300 g panko breadcrumbs

1 cup (250 ml) olive oil

lemon slices, to serve

garlic aioli, to serve

There's no denying that stuffing a zucchini flower is a tricky
business. It requires a certain amount of dexterity – and
patience. The fresher your flowers, the easier they will be to
handle, so if you aren't picking them fresh from the garden,
buy them on the day you intend eating them.

There are endless variations on the filling for this recipe: you
could try adding some Basil Pesto (see page 47), anchovies or
semi-dried tomatoes to this version if you like.

- In a bowl, mix together the ricotta, parmesan, capers and basil
  and season to taste with pepper.

- Gently open the zucchini flowers, taking care not to tear the
  petals. The fresher the flowers, the more easily they will open up.
  Holding a flower in one hand, carefully spoon in the filling until
  about three-quarters full – don't overfill or the flowers will tear
  and the filling will ooze out. Now fold the petals over the mixture
  to completely cover, then give the petals a little twist at the end
  to secure the filling. Repeat with the remaining flowers.

- Place the flour, beaten egg and breadcrumbs in separate shallow
  bowls. Gently dip the flowers and stalks into the flour, shaking
  off any excess, dip into the egg and then the breadcrumbs until
  they are well covered and transfer to a plate. Loosely cover with
  plastic film and place in the fridge for 30 minutes to firm.

- Heat the oil in a shallow frying pan over medium–high heat and
  fry the flowers for 3–5 minutes until they are crisp and golden.
  Be gentle as you turn them so no filling escapes. Drain on paper
  towel and serve immediately with a slice of lemon and some
  garlic aioli.

Risotto with zucchini flowers, peas and fresh pistachios

Serves 4

200 g peas in pod, to yield ½ cup (80 g) shelled peas

1 tablespoon olive oil

40 g butter

1 onion, finely chopped

1 clove organic garlic, finely chopped

1 cup (200 g) carnaroli or arborio rice

½ cup (125 ml) white wine

2½ cups (625 ml) hot chicken stock

4–5 zucchini (courgette) flowers and stalks, thinly sliced

3 tablespoons grated parmesan, plus extra to serve

¼ cup (35 g) fresh shelled pistachios, roughly chopped

salt and freshly ground black pepper

Fresh pistachios have a subtle flavour and a texture similar to fresh broad beans. I get mine from a grower in Coffs Harbour who has a stall at my local market, but they can be difficult to come by. If you get stumped, roasted unsalted pistachios are a good replacement.

You can use frozen peas if you can't get hold of fresh shelled peas for this.

- Blanch the peas by immersing them in just-boiled water for a moment, then transfer to a bowl of iced water. Leave them immersed for a minute or two, then drain and set aside.

- Heat the oil and half the butter in a heavy-based pan over medium heat. Add the onion and cook until soft and translucent. Add the garlic and gently fry for 1 minute. Add the rice and stir for 30 seconds until the grains are well coated in the mixture. Pour in the white wine and cook, stirring, until it has been absorbed. Turn the heat to low and add the hot stock, a ladleful at a time, gently stirring until each ladleful has been absorbed. This should take 15–20 minutes and the texture should be slightly sloppy. Add the sliced zucchini-flower stalks and cook for 5 minutes, then add the peas and stir just to heat them through. Turn off the heat, add the sliced zucchini flowers, parmesan, pistachios, some salt and pepper and the remaining butter and gently mix all the ingredients through.

- Serve immediately with extra cheese grated over the top.

Zucchini pickle

One of the problems you don't often have to deal with as a small-space gardener is a glut of produce: you usually only have enough room for a small crop. Some edibles, however, such as tomato and zucchini plants, can deliver very high yields. This is when you can transform your excess produce into preserves and pickles, and enjoy your spoils all through the year!

To sterilise jars and lids, I just put them through a normal wash cycle in my dishwasher. If you don't have a dishwasher, wash your jars and lids in hot soapy water, rinse thoroughly and place on a tray in a 140°C oven for 10 minutes.

Makes 2 cups

1 kg zucchinis (courgettes), chopped into 0.5 cm dice

2 large brown onions, finely chopped

1 red capsicum (pepper), seeds and white membrane removed, flesh finely chopped

3 tablespoons salt

2 cups (440 g) caster sugar

2 cups (500 ml) white vinegar, plus ⅓ cup (80 ml) extra

2 teaspoons mustard powder

2 teaspoons ground turmeric

2 teaspoons yellow mustard seeds

2 teaspoons cornflour

- Place the zucchini, onion and capsicum in a large non-reactive bowl, sprinkle with the salt and leave for 3 hours. Drain off any liquid.

- Combine the sugar, 2 cups vinegar, mustard powder, turmeric and mustard seeds in a large heavy-based saucepan and bring to the boil. Add the zucchini mixture, return to the boil and simmer for 25–30 minutes.

- Mix the cornflour with the extra vinegar and stir into the saucepan. Simmer for 2–3 minutes until the mixture thickens. While still hot, carefully spoon the mixture into sterilised jars and seal.

- This pickle can be eaten immediately or can be stored in the fridge for up to 12 months.

THE CHILLI PEPPERS DELAY THEIR APPEARANCE

The red horn pepper seeds I planted in late November were from the famous Italian seed company, Franchi. Summon all your patience for these: the first peppers didn't make an appearance until early March. My first crop stayed green, never turning red despite growing to the length of my hand. I'm not sure why this happened. They still tasted delicious but lacked that slightly punchy hit of flavour I was expecting.

This variety definitely needed staking. You'll need to insert the stakes as you plant your seedlings so you don't damage their root system: don't do as I did and put your stakes in when your plants are already 20 cm high! No doubt I damaged some important roots and this would have affected my pepper yields. My three plants were beaten about by some strong winds in early January, which caused quite a bit of blossom drop (which, in gardener's speak, means their flowers shrivelled and dropped off) and hence meant less fruit. Poor dears. I will shield them from the wind next time.

And in news just in – my last crop of late-season peppers has begun turning a deep fiery red. The first of the harvest made a delicious spicy salsa.

Red peppers

When to plant? Hot humid climate Year-round **Hot dry climate** July–December Cool temperate climate September–November

Seed or seedling? Will grow easily from both.

I like . . . full sun, well-draining soil.

I don't like . . . frosts; aphids.

Feed me . . . fortnightly with liquid fertiliser until fruit develops.

Give me a drink . . . every week, and more frequently during dry periods.

Pick me . . . from mid-summer onwards.

Roasted horn peppers with fetta

**It's not often that you literally find dinner growing on your balcony.
This recipe is so simple it almost cooks itself, and it's packed with flavour.
The horn peppers that I grow can be eaten green, or you can wait and pick
them when they turn red for a more robust flavour.**

Serves 6 as an entree or as part of a mezze platter

6 horn peppers

salt and freshly ground black pepper

sprinkling of dried Greek oregano

250 g Greek or Bulgarian fetta

extra virgin olive oil, for drizzling

lemon juice, finely peeled lemon zest and fresh oregano leaves, to garnish

- Roast the peppers on a barbecue or on the stove over a gas flame until the skins are
  blistered and blackened. Place the peppers in a sealed plastic bag and set aside for
  10 minutes – this will make it easier to remove the skins. Peel off as much blackened skin
  as you can, then make an incision lengthways along each pepper and scrape out the seeds
  and membranes. Don't be tempted to rinse them with water – you'll lose all the flavour.

- Sprinkle the inside of the peppers with salt, pepper and oregano, and place some fetta
  in each one. Close and drizzle with oil before topping with some lemon juice, zest and
  oregano, then scatter the remaining fetta on top. Serve just as they are for an entree,
  or as part of a mezze platter with olives and grilled bread.

Crumbed whiting with red pepper salsa

Serves 2

plain flour, for dusting

salt and freshly ground
black pepper

1 organic egg, beaten

1 cup panko breadcrumbs

4 whiting fillets

olive oil, for pan-frying

Red pepper salsa

2 red horn peppers, seeds
and white membrane
removed, flesh finely diced

1 red onion, finely diced

1 small clove organic
garlic, crushed

small handful flat-leaf
parsley leaves,
roughly chopped

1 tablespoon
extra virgin olive oil

1 teaspoon lemon juice

salt and freshly ground
black pepper

This recipe uses Japanese panko breadcrumbs, a larger, airier breadcrumb that gives a crunchier texture to fried dishes. You can buy them in good supermarkets, Asian food stores or specialty delis.

- Place the flour in a small bowl and season well. Place the beaten egg in a second bowl and the breadcrumbs in a third. Dust the whiting fillets with flour, then dip them in egg and finish with a coating of breadcrumbs. Put the fillets in the fridge to firm while you make the salsa.

- To make the salsa, place the diced pepper, onion, garlic, parsley, oil and lemon juice in a mixing bowl. Season with salt and pepper, then mix well and set aside for the flavours to infuse.

- Remove the fillets from the fridge and bring to room temperature. Heat some oil in a frying pan over medium heat and cook the fillets for 2–3 minutes on each side or until they are golden and crisp on both sides. Drain on paper towel.

- To serve, place two fillets on each plate and top with a generous spoonful of salsa.

69

TRANSFORMATION

I'm finding the process of gardening quite a revelation. Like a small child with building blocks, I can lose myself for hours potting new seedlings, watering the herbs or watching a bee collect some nectar. I don't know where the time goes. I see colours differently now. I notice how perfectly formed each leaf is, each flower. No two are the same. Every change my garden undergoes fills me with wonder and amazement. I feel truly engaged and connected with nature for possibly the first time. It may once have been a dull old balcony, but now it's the stage for Shakespearean-like epics. Everywhere I look there is birth, survival, sex, warfare, death and renewal. Who needs *Desperate Housewives*?

PEPPY MINT

As a child, I remember a huge mint bush always growing at the base of our garden tap. It was wonderful to wash your muddy hands under the cold running water and get a refreshing whiff of menthol at the same time. Mint, unlike its fellow herbs, loves having wet feet. It thrives in a damp, shady spot where it can send out its runners to colonise new territory. For this reason, it's best to grow mint in a container even if you do have a garden, as it can be invasive and will strangle other competing plants in its path.

There are so, so many varieties from which to choose, from the pungent, taper-leafed Vietnamese variety (which isn't actually a true mint, but a river weed) to the common mint. A pot of mint is essential on any edible balcony – how could you throw together those refreshing summer cocktails without it?

Common mint

When to plant? Hot humid climate Year-round Hot dry climate July–April
Cool temperate climate August–March

Seed or seedling? Seedling.

I like . . . damp soil and partial shade. Can sprawl and take over the garden so always grow in a pot.

I don't like . . . drying out; caterpillars.

Feed me . . . liquid fertiliser every month.

Give me a drink . . . frequently.

Pick me . . . as needed, or to control sprawl.

Mojito cocktail

**In the late 1990s, Sydney's hippest bar was The International in Kings Cross.
I'd sometimes drop in for a nightcap on the way home after presenting the
late-night news on SBS. This was where I tried my first mojito cocktail
and they've been my weakness ever since.**

**If you don't have a muddler on hand to crush your lime wedges,
use the end of a rolling pin or the handle of a wooden spoon.**

Makes 1

10 mint leaves, plus extra to serve

½ lime, cut into four wedges

2 tablespoons caster sugar

ice cubes

45 ml white rum

½ cup (125 ml) soda water

- Place the mint leaves and one lime wedge in a tall glass and crush with a muddler to release the oils and juices. Add the sugar and two more lime wedges, then crush again. Do not strain the mixture.

- Fill the glass almost to the top with ice. Pour rum over the ice, then fill the glass with soda water. Garnish with the remaining lime wedge and extra mint leaves.

Peking duck and Vietnamese mint rice paper rolls

Serves 4 as an entree

12 large round rice
paper wrappers

½ Chinese roast duck, meat
and crispy skin removed
from bones and thinly sliced

1 Lebanese cucumber, sliced
into 10 cm × 0.5 cm strips

½ cup (75 g) chopped
roasted unsalted peanuts

24 Vietnamese mint leaves,
12 finely chopped and
12 left whole

2 tablespoons
chopped coriander

1 tablespoon hoisin sauce

Dipping sauce

2 tablespoons grated
palm sugar

2 tablespoons lime juice

1 chilli, seeds removed,
finely chopped

1 tablespoon
chopped coriander

I once saw rice paper being made by a Vietnamese villager on a television cooking show and it was a process that required extraordinary skill. He poured the thin ground-rice batter onto a hot stone and then gently peeled away the crisp semi-translucent film to be dried on grass wall-racks. Luckily, rice paper can be bought ready-made, making these rolls a quick and simple snack or entree.

- Line a dinner plate with a damp tea towel. Fill a large bowl with hot water and dip in a rice paper wrapper until softened, then transfer it to the lined dinner plate. Repeat with the remaining wrappers, being careful not to tear them.

- Lay out a softened wrapper on a clean benchtop. In the centre of the wrapper, place some duck meat and crispy skin, cucumber, peanuts, chopped mint and coriander. Drizzle over some hoisin sauce and top with a mint leaf. Take the edge of the rice wrapper closest to you and fold it tightly over the filling, then tuck in the sides and roll up very firmly into a cigar shape. Use a little water if needed to seal the edge. Repeat with the remaining wrappers.

- To make the dipping sauce, mix all the ingredients together in a small bowl.

- Serve the rice paper rolls immediately with the dipping sauce alongside.

Vietnamese mint

When to plant? Hot humid climate Year-round **Hot dry climate** Year-round
Cool temperate climate October–December

Seed or seedling? Seedling.

I like . . . a shaded spot, though will tolerate full shade, or full sun in cooler regions.

I don't like . . . frosts, but will recover in warmer weather; slugs.

Feed me . . . liquid fertiliser every month.

Give me a drink . . . frequently – a thirsty drinker.

Pick me . . . as leaves mature. Regular harvesting will encourage a bushier plant.

FLOWER POWER

I planted my nasturtiums in woven hanging baskets suspended along the balcony railing by large steel bicycle-storage hooks (these handy hooks are available from large hardware stores). This way, the nasturtiums can sprawl and twist along the balcony railing, and any run-off drips onto the plants below, thereby saving water.

I'm growing nasturtiums for many reasons. Firstly, they're edible. Not just the flowers, but the leaves, flower buds and seeds as well. I planted my nasturtium seeds in late September and had flowers by early December. As soon as the plants started bulking up and spreading, I began picking the leaves, flowers and flower buds. You can add the flowers to dips, pesto, spreads and cream cheese for added flavour and visual appeal (but be careful when serving flowers as pollen traces may affect asthmatics). The flower buds can be pickled like capers and the leaves have a pungent peppery flavour that can enhance many salads and dishes. Mature seeds, when dried, can be ground and used as a pepper substitute for seasoning.

Secondly, nasturtiums are little apothecary masters as well. They are high in vitamin C, iron and other minerals, and also have powerful antimicrobial and antioxidant qualities. For this reason, I like to chew on a few leaves or buds each day while I'm watering the garden.

But wait – there's more. Nasturtiums also make good companion plants, as they excrete a strong pungent essence which has been found to deter aphids, white fly and root pests. This essence, when secreted into the soil, is absorbed by other plants, helping them also to resist attacks from pests and disease (see page 24 for more information on companion planting). Some gardeners make their own aphid spray with nasturtium leaves by infusing them in boiling water, with a little liquid soap added if you like, then cooling and straining them. You can use it immediately or store in a cool dry place.

But the best thing about having nasturtiums on my balcony is that their beautiful variegated leaves and bright open faces make me feel happy.

Chives

When to plant? Hot humid climate Year-round **Hot dry climate** July–April
Cool temperate climate August–March

Seed or seedling? Either: sow seed directly into pots or buy seedlings from garden centres year-round.

I like . . . moist, well-draining soil in a sunny position.

I don't like . . . drying out.

Feed me . . . liquid fertiliser every month.

Give me a drink . . . frequently in hot weather.

Pick me . . . as needed; will regrow new shoots.

COME ALIVE WITH CHIVES

One of the discoveries you'll make when you grow your own herbs is how much more pungent they are. The flavour of my home-grown chives is almost as strong as the red shallots I use in my Thai curry pastes: they kick arse. No mistaking them for the packets of 'grass' you buy at the supermarket.

And chives are so versatile. They enhance any dish with eggs, go wonderfully with curd cheeses and lift seafood, such as salmon, to sublime heights. They're a hardy perennial and grow right back after a haircut. And like other members of the onion family, there's no holding them back. Mine are loving their spot on the vertical herb wall (more on this on page 141), where they get a half-day of shade and a half-day of light. They're doing just dandy.

Summer on the edible balcony has seen my gardening skill-level move from that of 'heightened panic' to a slightly more relaxed 'wary vigilance'. Somehow I've managed to grow things – from delicate herbs to trombone-sized zucchinis. And most rewarding of all is that they've tasted better than any produce I've eaten before. I could get used to this.

I wonder what the autumn winds will blow in?

Crepes with smoked salmon, caviar, creme fraiche and chives

Serves 8 as an appetiser

250 g creme fraiche

20 slices smoked salmon

1 cup finely chopped chives

2 tablespoons salmon caviar, to garnish (optional)

Crepes

1 cup (150 g) plain flour

pinch of salt

1 organic egg

1½ cups (375 ml) milk

butter, for pan-frying

Smoked salmon, creme fraiche and chives are a sublime food match. These little canapes can be prepared on the morning of your summer soiree and sliced just before serving. You'll be the hostess with the mostest.

- To make the crepes, sift the flour and salt into a bowl and make a well in the centre. Add the egg and mix with a wooden spoon, then gradually whisk in the milk, a little at a time, until you have a smooth batter. Strain the mixture into a jug and allow to rest for 30 minutes, after which the batter should resemble the consistency of pouring cream; if it is a little thick, add some more milk.

- Heat a crepe pan or small frying pan over medium heat and grease with a little butter on a paper towel. Pour in enough batter to just cover the surface of the pan with a thin film and cook for 2 minutes or until the edges become crisp. Carefully turn the crepe over and cook for about 20 seconds on the other side. Slide the crepe onto a plate and repeat with the remaining batter; you should have enough batter to make eight crepes.

- Place a crepe on a clean benchtop and spread evenly with creme fraiche. Take care as the crepes are delicate and can tear easily. Cover completely with a thin layer of smoked salmon and a sprinkling of chopped chives, reserving some chives to use as a garnish. Roll the crepe into a tight log and wrap firmly in plastic film. Repeat with the remaining crepes and filling, then refrigerate for about an hour.

- When ready to serve, unwrap the crepes and slice each log into discs 2–3 cm thick. Arrange on a serving platter, top with a final sprinkling of chives, and add some salmon caviar, if using, for an extra bit of indulgence.

ROSEMARY

EGGPLANT

SPRING ONIONS

CHILLIES

CORIANDER

PEAS

THYME

BORAGE

RAINBOW SILVER

BOK CHOY

TATSOI

PAK CHOY

AUTUMN

Ah, autumn . . . the mornings are a golden buzz of light and warmth, and the air still smells of summer holidays — sea, salt and zinc cream.

AUTUMN TENANTS

It's the first crisp day of autumn. Sunshine bounces off the harbour like thousands of scattered diamonds while hard-working ferries chug back and forth to Circular Quay. From my vantage point I have a bird's-eye view of commuters scurrying down the road to their grey offices, their faces frozen with dread and boredom – their summer break now but a distant memory. At least I have the edible balcony – a little bit of holiday that never goes away.

I've mellowed with the change in season. Gone is my hyper, new-mother over-attentiveness. I'm beginning to realise that sometimes you just have to let your plants be and, like a baby's cry, they will let you know when they need something. Cold? Their leaves will curl. Too wet or dry? They might turn brown or yellow. When they need a feed, they'll look listless and flat, and when they need a nappy change – well, you could quite possibly have a new plant species on your hands.

My autumn plantings are already in: broccoli, peas, spring onions, carrots, chillies, borage, rosemary, parsley, thyme, coriander and garlic. The dreamer in me wishes I had room to experiment with more varieties. Another voice in my head (sounding remarkably like Mark's) tells me to get a grip – I'll be pushing it just to get this lot over the line. Ah, the gardener's constant dilemma: so much to grow, so little room in which to do it. More importantly, will I be up to the challenges this season will throw at me, or will Mother Nature finally vote me off the balcony?

LITTLE MISS EGGPLANT

We all have a high-maintenance friend who is constantly embroiled in some drama involving work or a boyfriend or a parent (heck – some of us *are* that friend!). They sap our emotional energy and if they weren't so attractive, we would have dropped them ages ago. Ladies and gentlemen, meet the drama queen of the vegetable world: Little Miss Eggplant. Beautiful she may be on the outside, but a 'me, me, me' attention-seeker she is all the same. Tempted by her dark sultry curves and juicy voluptuous flesh, the novice balcony gardener is in for a roller-coaster ride with this relationship.

My romance with three long purple eggplants started smoothly enough. I planted them in November and they germinated from seed without incident. By late December I had culled one plant to give the others more room. Then, as soon as the first leaves appeared, I noticed some tiny white-winged beetles hanging around. They seemed harmless enough, but by the next day my eggplant leaves were webs of lace, and I soon discovered I had a serious case of flea beetle. I hand-squished as many as I could there and then, and began a round-the-clock vigil.

There were hundreds of them. As soon as I destroyed one, ten more seemed to hatch in their place. I was feverish with determination. I wasn't going to let a few bugs get between me and my moussaka. My persistence eventually paid off. The flea beetles had been beat. But then within a few days, with the eggplants in an already weakened state, hordes of opportunistic aphids and mealy bugs swarmed all over the new flower shoots. Pest oil wasn't making any inroads so in desperation I turned to Google. And there it was – the answer to my prayers – a company that bred predator insects that fed on aphids and mealy bugs but didn't eat your plants. Based in Queensland, Bugs for Bugs (*bugsforbugs.com.au*) would even mail the little critters to me.

Three days later, a courier arrived with my tiny terminators. There, in little plastic containers nestled in shredded paper, were about 100 native ladybirds and 100 green lacewing larvae, dazed but hungry and ready to get to work.

'Boys, the all-you-can-eat buffet is this way!'

During the next two days they hoovered up every aphid and mealy bug on the eggplant leaves with genocidal precision. It was shock and awe. But unlike a US military operation, there was no collateral damage. They left the eggplant buds and leaves intact. And when their food source was gone, so were my terminators. Within minutes of the last aphid being devoured, they had flown away to seek out greener pastures. My bugs came with a hefty $40 price tag, but left no damaging chemical or ecological footprint in their wake. That was important to me. I'd also helped release more good bugs into an urban ecosystem that sorely needed them. And who knows, their offspring may just pay me a visit later when I need them.

As a result of their harrowing gestation, the five eggplants that managed to develop were very special indeed. My smooth, dark-skinned, shiny beauties were perfection, expensive perfection. They made a moussaka to die for.

Eggplant

When to plant? Hot humid climate Year-round **Hot dry climate** September–December **Cool temperate climate** September–November

Seed or seedling? Seed. Sow in punnets and transfer to a pot after 4–6 weeks.

I like . . . rich soil containing rotted manure and compost. Need a long period of warm weather to mature.

I don't like . . . cold weather; aphids and flea beetles.

Feed me . . . liquid fertiliser once a month.

Give me a drink . . . regularly.

Pick me . . . when fruit is glossy.

Eggplant moussaka stacks

Serves 4

4 eggplants (aubergines), cut into 3 cm-thick rounds

salt

2 tablespoons olive oil, plus extra for grilling and drizzling

1 large brown onion, chopped

4 cloves organic garlic, crushed

¼ teaspoon ground cinnamon

¼ teaspoon grated nutmeg

500 g minced lamb

½ cup (125 ml) red wine

1 × 400 g can chopped tomatoes

small handful flat-leaf parsley leaves, chopped

1 teaspoon grated lemon zest

freshly ground black pepper

basil leaves, to serve

⅓ cup (25 g) grated parmesan (optional)

Bechamel sauce

30 g unsalted butter

60 g plain flour

1½ cups (375 ml) milk

sprinkle of grated nutmeg

salt and freshly ground white pepper

Traditional moussakas can be very rich and filling. I like this pared-back version because it cuts down on the heaviness and the cooking time, and – served with a Greek salad – makes a stylish meal for a dinner party.

- Sprinkle the eggplant slices on both sides with salt and set aside in a colander to drain for 30 minutes. This will draw out any bitterness.

- Heat the oil in a large heavy-based saucepan over medium heat. Add the onion and cook for 10 minutes until it is just beginning to colour. Add the garlic, cinnamon and nutmeg and cook for 1 minute, then add the minced lamb and cook for 8–10 minutes or until browned. Pour in the wine and cook for about 10 minutes or until the liquid has reduced by half, then add the tomato, parsley, lemon zest and salt and pepper to taste. Reduce heat to low and cook for 30 minutes until the sauce has thickened.

- Meanwhile, to make the bechamel sauce, melt the butter in a small saucepan, then add the flour and stir until a thick paste forms. Gradually add the milk, whisking as you go, being careful not to let any lumps form. Continue cooking until the sauce thickens and coats the back of a spoon (this should take about 8–10 minutes). Add the nutmeg and adjust the seasoning with salt and pepper.

- Carefully wipe off any excess salt and moisture from the eggplant slices using paper towel. Preheat a barbecue or chargrill plate to medium–high. Brush the eggplant with olive oil and grill for 2–3 minutes on each side until soft and cooked through.

- To assemble, layer a slice of eggplant with meat sauce, a few basil leaves and some bechamel, and top with another eggplant slice. Continue layering until you have a stack four slices high, then repeat with the rest of the ingredients to make four stacks in all.

- Serve warm topped with grated parmesan, if using, and a drizzle of olive oil.

Spicy eggplant fritters

**Crank these out when you have hordes to feed. The eggplant becomes soft
and creamy; a wonderful contrast to the spicy crunchy batter.**

Makes 20

2 cups (300 g) chickpea flour (besan flour)

1 teaspoon baking powder

1 teaspoon mild chilli powder

½ teaspoon ground turmeric

1 teaspoon ground cumin seeds

1 teaspoon ground fennel seeds

1 teaspoon salt, plus extra for serving

2 cups (500 ml) vegetable oil, for frying

2 large eggplants (aubergines), cut into 1 cm-thick rounds

- Sift the chickpea flour, baking powder, chilli powder, turmeric, cumin, fennel and salt into
  a wide, shallow bowl. Add some water, a little at a time, stirring between each addition,
  until you have a batter slightly thicker than the consistency of pouring cream (you'll need
  about ¾ cup water). If the batter is too runny, it won't stick to the eggplant; too thick and
  it will absorb too much oil.

- Heat the oil in a deep heavy-based frying pan over medium–high heat. Working in batches,
  dip the eggplant slices in batter until well coated and fry for about 4 minutes on each side
  until the batter is lightly puffed and golden and the eggplant is soft. Drain on paper towel,
  then sprinkle with salt and serve hot.

LONG PURPLE
EGGPLANT

Pak choy, bok choy, tatsoi

When to plant? Hot humid climate March–May Hot dry climate February–May
Cool temperate climate February–March

Seed or seedling? Grows best from seed sown in cooler months.

I like . . . plenty of compost and rotted manure; full sun.

I don't like . . . drying out; snails and slugs.

Feed me . . . liquid fertiliser fortnightly after seedlings reach 15 cm in height.

Give me a drink . . . regularly to maintain rapid growth.

Pick me . . . pick whole plants as needed.

EAT YOUR GREENS

Like Popeye, my biceps start bulging at the sight of fresh, leafy greens. I love them for their high levels of antioxidants and vitamins; they're like green pseudoephedrine to me. Happily, their delicious taste is an added bonus.

Most greens require the same conditions to flourish – well-draining soil, less sunlight than most edibles (four–five hours per day), and regular doses of liquid nitrogen fertiliser to keep their leaves bushy and crunchy. The shallow root systems of most greens mean they can adapt to almost any soil depth, so they don't require much space or soil. I put mine in 30 cm-deep pots and 10 cm-deep hanging baskets. Greens will use up as much room as you give them. Pack them in and they will sprout a stalk and grow up. Give them space and they will fan out at ground level, especially the Chinese greens.

Their leaves have such an interesting variety of textures and patterns that they also have wonderful ornamental appeal as well – especially when backlit with balcony sunshine. The pak choy and tatsoi I planted threw up strong, sturdy leaves; the leaves of the rainbow silverbeet were so resilient they were almost rubber-like in texture. Greens also seem to thrive from inattention. On a balcony, few bugs can attack them and those that do can be easily contained with – yes, you guessed it – a few squirts of pest oil.

Greens begin losing their nutritional value as soon as they are picked, so if you buy those limp bunches from the supermarket you may as well be eating lawn clippings. The wonderful advantage of having your own greens patch is that you can pick only as many leaves as you need, maximising freshness and minimising waste. For a quick lunch, I like stir-frying my greens with onions, garlic, some mustard seeds and a few chilli flakes and then lightly stirring through a beaten egg.

Rainbow silverbeet

When to plant? Hot humid climate Year-round Hot dry climate July–March
Cool temperate climate August–February

Seed or seedling? Either.

I like . . . full sun and fertile, well-draining soil. Dig in plenty of compost and well-rotted manure.

I don't like . . . drying out, or will bolt; snails and slugs.

Feed me . . . liquid fertiliser every fortnight.

Give me a drink . . . regularly, especially in summer.

Pick me . . . regularly or as needed, starting with the outer leaves. Harvesting will encourage growth.

Pork wonton soup with tatsoi

**Tatsoi is a type of Chinese cabbage that grows in pretty rosettes.
Its leaves are thick and spoon-like and make a very attractive edible plant.
It is packed with calcium and minerals so it's best eaten quickly
blanched to retain most of its nutrients.**

Serves 4

250 g minced pork

4 spring onions, green and white parts finely sliced

3 tablespoons grated ginger

2 tablespoons soy sauce

2 tablespoons chopped coriander leaves, plus extra to garnish

25 wonton wrappers

1.25 litres chicken stock

10–15 tatsoi leaves

sliced red chilli, to garnish

- In a large bowl, combine the minced pork with the spring onion, ginger, soy sauce and coriander.

- Take a wonton wrapper and place a teaspoon of this mixture in the centre. Brush the edges with a little water and fold diagonally to form a triangle. Seal the edges by pressing firmly. Repeat using all the wrappers and mixture – you should have enough to make 20–25 wontons.

- In a large heavy-based pan, bring the chicken stock to the boil over high heat then reduce to a simmer over medium heat. Add the tatsoi leaves and gently drop in the wontons. Cook for 3–4 minutes or until cooked through.

- To serve, ladle the broth and wontons into bowls and garnish with sliced red chilli and extra coriander.

Poached sesame chicken on wilted pak choy

Serves 2

2 skinless chicken breast fillets (about 300 g)

10 pak choy leaves, washed

1 teaspoon toasted white sesame seeds

steamed rice, to serve (optional)

Master stock

½ cup (125 ml) Chinese shaohsing rice wine

3 cloves organic garlic, crushed

2 tablespoons honey

5 cm piece ginger

3 tablespoons soy sauce

1 cup (250 ml) chicken stock

2 star anise

1 spring onion, green and white parts sliced

Many Chinese recipes call for a master stock, made using wonderful aromatics that impart a deeply perfumed flavour and deep-red colour to the dish. Some Chinese families keep their master stock for years in the freezer, boiling and straining it with each use to remove particles that could cause the growth of harmful bacteria.

If you're buying ready-made chicken stock for this, try and get the salt-reduced version to compensate for the saltiness of the soy sauce. If you're making your own, there's no need to add any salt.

- Place all the stock ingredients in a large heavy-based pot and simmer over low heat for 40 minutes. Gently lower the chicken into the stock and poach for 8–10 minutes or until just cooked through, then remove the chicken from the stock with tongs, slice thickly and set aside in a warm place.

- Increase the heat to high and boil the stock for about 10 minutes until the liquid has reduced by half. Add the pak choy leaves and blanch for 2–3 minutes until wilted, then drain the leaves, reserving the stock.

- Pile the steamed pak choy onto plates, then arrange the chicken on top, spooning over some stock and scattering over the white sesame seeds. Serve with steamed rice if you like.

Rainbow silverbeet and fetta spanakopita serpent

Serves 4 as a main or 8 as part of a mezze platter

1 tablespoon olive oil, plus extra for brushing

500 g rainbow silverbeet (swiss chard), leaves and stalks finely chopped

20 g unsalted butter, plus extra, melted, for brushing

1 large onion, finely chopped

2 cloves organic garlic, finely chopped

200 g fetta, crumbled

⅓ cup (50 g) pine nuts, toasted

3 organic eggs, beaten

½ teaspoon sugar (optional)

6 sheets filo pastry, thawed if frozen

3 teaspoons caraway seeds

When you grow your own rainbow silverbeet (or swiss chard as it is also known), you'll discover that the larger leaves have a stronger, more astringent taste than the smaller ones. Large leaves need to be cooked, while only the very young, small leaves can be eaten raw. If cooking does bring out the bitterness in your silverbeet, I've suggested adding a touch of sugar to the filling. Of course, plain white-stalked silverbeet can be used in this recipe if you can't get the rainbow variety.

- Preheat fan-forced oven to 180°C and grease a round baking tray or a baking sheet.

- Heat the oil in a large frying pan over low heat and fry the silverbeet stalks for 10 minutes or until tender. Add the leaves and cook until wilted and all the liquid in the pan has evaporated. Transfer to a bowl and set aside.

- In the same pan, melt the butter then cook the onion for 10 minutes or until soft. Add the garlic and stir for a minute until fragrant. Transfer the onion and garlic to the bowl with the silverbeet, then stir in the fetta, pine nuts and beaten egg. Taste the mixture – if it's a little bitter, add a sprinkling of sugar and stir through.

- Lay out one sheet of filo on a clean benchtop and brush with olive oil. Spread a long thin sausage of filling along one side and roll up into a cigar shape. Repeat with remaining filling and filo sheets.

- Arrange the filo rolls in a snake-like coil on the baking tray or sheet, leaving a little room between the coils for the pastry to rise. Brush with melted butter, sprinkle with caraway seeds and bake for 20–25 minutes until the pastry is crisp and golden.

- Serve cut into small lengths.

NOT SO EASY-PEASY

Peas were the first vegetable my parents encouraged me to grow as a child – probably because I refused to eat them. I would pick the peas out of every meal and carefully arrange them into a pea necklace around the edge of my dinner plate.

Tending to my own pea patch soon converted me: peas are usually easy to grow and kids will eat almost anything they've nurtured. Now I can't imagine ever not liking them.

Peas are legumes and therefore fix nitrogen from the air into the soil, improving soil quality and giving a nutrient boost to other nearby plants. Fresh peas are at their most sweet and delicious picked straight off the vine and popped straight into your mouth, before their natural sugars start converting to starch. In fact, most of my home-grown peas never even made it to the kitchen.

I chose a yellow-podded heirloom variety for my balcony crop. The seed packet boasted that the pod was edible as well: great, I thought, a double bang for my buck. According to the instructions, they were best planted autumn to spring, so I buried eight seeds into a rectangular fibreglass pot in early April. I employed some of my little-used Girl Guide skills to build a little teepee from stakes tied together with string to give the peas a climbing frame. My crop in early August was delicious but small (about twenty pods in all), but soon, one by one, the leaves started developing a fine white dust, then turned yellow. Powdery mildew had taken hold, probably due to the lingering warm summer weather we had, which may not have suited this variety's temperate sensibilities.

Next time, I'm going to plant later in the season and try a common pea variety that may be a little more robust. Just goes to show, it's never easy being green – especially when you are a pea (or Bob Brown).

Peas

When to plant? Hot humid climate March–July Hot dry climate February–August Cool temperate climate July–September

Seed or seedling? Plant seeds in damp soil with some lime and well-rotted manure. Don't water again until seeds have emerged.

I like . . . mulching; wire frames or trellises to climb.

I don't like . . . getting damp; snails and slugs.

Feed me . . . when planting.

Give me a drink . . . pea seeds are prone to rot, so water well when planting and again after germination.

Pick me . . . 9–12 weeks after planting.

Pea, pancetta, pea shoot and rocket salad

Peas begin converting their sugars into powdery starch very soon after they ripen, which is why home-grown peas picked straight from the vine are so much sweeter than supermarket ones. You can also use frozen peas in this recipe (blanch them for 2 minutes in just-boiled water, then refresh them in iced water).

Serves 2 as a main or 4 as a side dish

200 g pancetta, cut into short lengths

400 g peas in pod, to yield 1 cup (160 g) shelled peas

3 handfuls rocket leaves

handful pea shoots

100 g fetta, crumbled

1 tablespoon sherry vinegar

freshly ground black pepper

mint leaves, to garnish

- Fry the pancetta in a frying pan for about 10 minutes until crisp and browned. Remove the pan from the heat and stir through the peas.

- Place the rocket leaves in a large salad bowl. Remove the peas and pancetta from the frying pan with a slotted spoon and add to the bowl; pour the pan juices into a jar with a screw-top lid and set aside. Add the pea shoots and fetta to the bowl and mix the ingredients gently.

- Add the vinegar and pepper to the jar and shake to combine. Pour the dressing over the salad and give another gentle toss. Garnish with mint leaves and serve.

THE BROCCOLI BLUES

A poorly timed overseas trip has cost me my broccoli crop. Unable to monitor its progress while I was away, it's gone to flower and seed before I could taste even one floret. This phenomenon is known as bolting, and could have been caused by too much direct sun or a lack of water. It's emotionally challenging dealing with this failure. I had been lulled into a false sense of competency by so many successes during summer so The Great Broccoli Bolt leaves me shattered. Boo hoo. I have the broccoli blues. I did, however, make a discovery for all those florists out there: broccoli flowers are simply breathtaking. Their delicate, buttercup-yellow petals were a partial compensation.

We went to a restaurant to get my mind off my post-boltal depression. When a side dish of bright chlorophyll-green, steaming broccoli came out with my meal, I let out a shuddering sob.

Mark says I'll be fine after some therapy.

IT'S CHILLI WHEN IT'S HOT

Given my South African–Indian heritage, people are often surprised at how little chilli I eat. I don't overly enjoy big blow-your-head-off chilli hits like some chilli lovers do. I seek out chillies with a rounded spicy flavour that add warmth rather than heat. For this reason I'm growing a Thai Silk chilli variety that hits about halfway on the Scoville heat scale when the chilli is very ripe and red. As the fruit on this variety develops, it changes colour from white to cream to pale yellow to orange, then mauve to purple and finally to fire-engine red. A rainbow in a pot. The chillies can be used at any stage during their fruiting according to the intensity of heat you desire. If you just want a mild chilli hit, pick a yellow or orange one. If you want a bang, go for the red ones.

My chilli plant is enjoying its position in full sun on the balcony, but I still need to give it a squirt occasionally with pest oil to keep those dreaded aphids at bay. When plants taste this good, can you blame them?

Chillies

When to plant? Hot humid climate Year-round Hot dry climate July–December Cool temperate climate September–November

Seed or seedling? Grows easily from both.

I like . . . full sun and well-draining soil.

I don't like . . . frosts; aphids.

Feed me . . . liquid fertiliser fortnightly until the plant develops fruit.

Give me a drink . . . occasionally during dry periods.

Pick me . . . from mid-summer onwards.

Flat-leaf parsley

When to plant? Hot humid climate Year-round Hot dry climate August–May
Cool temperate climate September–April

Seed or seedling? Grows best from seed. Soak seed before planting to speed up germination (which can take up to 28 days).

I like . . . full sun or semi-shade; well-draining, fertile soil.

I don't like . . . being planted from seedling (may suffer 'transplant shock'); aphids.

Feed me . . . liquid fertiliser fortnightly – loves being fed!

Give me a drink . . . occasionally, although really thirsty in summer.

Pick me . . . as required.

PASS THE PARSLEY

Parsley could quite possibly be the most versatile of all the herbs, particularly the flat-leaf (or continental) variety. There is rarely a savoury dish I prepare that can't be enhanced by the addition of parsley. Its papery, maple-leaf-shaped leaves can be finely chopped and added to soups, casseroles or sauces, or torn off whole to add to a green salad or panzanella. Or they can become a star in their own right in a tabbouleh or a salsa verde, a green sauce that goes beautifully with fish and barbecued meat. The bigger the pot in which you plant it, the bigger your parsley bush will grow. So if you are as keen on parsley as I am, give it room to spread its wings. It likes a sunny spot, with well-draining soil and a regular feed of liquid fertiliser to encourage lush foliage.

Indira's cure-all chicken soup with chilli and parsley

Serves 4

1 tablespoon olive oil

1 tablespoon ghee

4 cloves organic garlic, crushed

5 cm piece young ginger, finely chopped

1 sprig thyme

1 dried bay leaf

½ teaspoon dried chilli flakes

2 carrots, diced

1 litre good-quality chicken stock

1 cup (250 ml) boiling water

2 large potatoes, diced

2 skinless chicken breast fillets (about 300 g), roughly diced

small handful flat-leaf parsley leaves, roughly chopped

salt and freshly ground black pepper

buttered toast soldiers, to serve (optional)

Every culture seems to have its own version of chicken soup. The healing power of this dish isn't just an old wives' tale: it's based on medical fact. Apparently, cooking chicken releases an amino acid that helps ease respiratory problems, and the spices used, such as garlic and pepper, work the same way as cough medicines, thinning mucus and making breathing easier. When I get a distress call from fluey friends and family, a bowl of this chicken soup is what Nurse Naidoo always prescribes.

- Heat the oil and ghee in a large heavy-based saucepan over low heat. Add the garlic, ginger, thyme, bay leaf and chilli flakes and cook for 5 minutes until aromatic.

- Add the carrot and cook for 2 minutes. Pour in the stock and boiling water and stir. Add the potato, bring to the boil and then simmer until the potato is just soft. Add the chicken and cook for 2–3 minutes or until just cooked.

- Remove the pan from the heat, cover and leave to stand for 10 minutes. Stir in the parsley, season with salt and pepper and serve with hot buttered toast soldiers, if you like.

THE EDIBLE BALCONY

HAPPY BEDFELLOWS

I've planted my carrots and the spring onions together in the same pot because they're meant to be great companions. These buddies apparently love to grow in close proximity – the spring onions keep the bugs away from the carrots, and the carrots excrete trace elements into the soil that fortify the onions. The carrot seeds are an heirloom French variety called St Valery, famed for its sweetness. They need about eighty days to mature, so at least there'll be something bright and delicious to look forward to in winter.

The spring onions are also growing from seed but much more quickly; I can begin picking their long tapered shoots after about six weeks while they are still fine and young. They give a wonderful subtle hint of onion flavour to salads and Asian dishes.

Spring onions

When to plant? Hot humid climate March–November Hot dry climate Year-round Cool temperate climate Year-round

Seed or seedling? Seed.

I like . . . well-draining soil, with compost.

I don't like . . . hot, humid conditions; aphids.

Feed me . . . with a non-nitrogen fertiliser once a week after germination.

Give me a drink . . . regularly, and more often in summer.

Pick me . . . as needed.

IT'S THYME

Some people have comfort foods, I have a comfort herb: thyme. I find it so soothing snapping off a sprig of thyme, rubbing its leaves gently between my fingers, closing my eyes and inhaling deeply. Thyme's aromatic woodiness is connected to all my fondest food memories – thyme and butter melting over crispy roast chicken, thyme gently frying in olive oil for Mum's lamb stew, or thyme tossed with braised pork and potatoes with spaghetti. It's a delight to grow, quietly accumulating flavour in its tiny spiky leaves through all weather conditions.

Thyme is a great herb to use dried as well as fresh, although you only need to use about half as much as the flavour is much stronger. Dry your fresh thyme by hanging it in bunches in a dry, shady spot, then once dried you can pick the leaves from the sprigs and store in the pantry in an airtight container.

Crispy Lebanese bread with olive oil and za'atar

This recipe uses sumac, an exotic Middle Eastern spice that combines magically with dried thyme to create za'atar. Sumac comes from a crimson-coloured berry that has a fruity, lemon-like tanginess and can be found at good spice stores.

Serves 4 as part of a mezze platter

1 teaspoon sesame seeds

1½ tablespoons dried thyme leaves

2 teaspoons sumac

½ teaspoon salt

4 slices Lebanese bread

olive oil, for brushing

- Preheat fan-forced oven to 180°C.

- Dry-fry the sesame seeds over low heat in a small frying pan until fragrant and lightly coloured, then set aside. Crush the dried thyme leaves using a mortar and pestle. Add the sumac, toasted sesame seeds and salt and crush until a rough powdery paste is formed.

- Brush each piece of Lebanese bread generously on one side with olive oil, then spread the za'atar evenly on top. Bake for 8–10 minutes until the bread is slightly brown and crisp, then remove from the oven and allow to cool (they will crisp further as they cool).

Fig, blue cheese, thyme and wild honey tart

Don't be afraid to experiment with your balcony herbs in desserts as well; this tart brings together the complementary flavours of figs, blue cheese and thyme for an earthy dessert. Buy the best wild honey you can find, not the diluted type sold in plastic squeezable containers from the supermarket.

Serves 8

3 square sheets ready-rolled puff pastry, thawed if frozen

300 g gorgonzola dolce (a mild blue cheese), crumbled

⅓ cup (80 ml) wild honey

small handful fresh thyme leaves

1 organic egg, lightly beaten

10 figs, thinly sliced lengthways

salt and freshly ground black pepper

- Preheat fan-forced oven to 200°C and grease a 40 cm × 25 cm baking sheet.

- Cut one square sheet of pastry in half, and join one piece to a full square of pastry to make a sheet large enough to fit the tray. Repeat with the other half.

- Lay one of the large pastry sheets on the tray and spread evenly with cheese, leaving a 1 cm border around the edge. Drizzle over a third of the wild honey and half the thyme. Brush the edges with beaten egg, then place the other large sheet of pastry on top and press down gently just along the edges to seal.

- Brush the top with more beaten egg and top with the fig slices. Sprinkle over the rest of the thyme and season with salt and pepper. Bake for about 20 minutes until the pastry is puffed and golden. If the centre of the tart is still a little uncooked, cover the ends with foil to stop them burning and bake for a further 5 minutes.

- Drizzle evenly with the rest of the honey and serve warm.

Grilled scallops on thyme skewers

My thyme plant is now about five years old and grows quite long woody sprigs. These make perfect skewers for little morsels of grilled meat and vegetables while imparting the food with wonderful flavour. If you don't have thyme sprigs long enough, sprinkle some thyme leaves into the marinade and use metal skewers instead.

Serves 4 as a canape

16 scallops, cleaned and trimmed

2 tablespoons fresh orange juice

2 teaspoons fresh lime juice

2 teaspoons chopped lemon zest

8 long sprigs thyme

olive oil, for brushing

salt and freshly ground black pepper

- Carefully slice the scallops in half, creating two thin discs (unless they are small scallops, in which case leave them whole). Place them in a bowl with the orange and lime juices and the lemon zest and marinate for 1 hour.

- Meanwhile, prepare the thyme skewers by pulling the leaves off the sprigs, leaving a few leaves at one end. Cut the end of the sprigs diagonally to create a sharp point; this will make it easier to thread the scallop pieces.

- Preheat a barbecue grill plate to high. Thread two scallop pieces onto each thyme sprig, brush with olive oil and sprinkle with salt and pepper. Cook for 10 seconds on each side on the hot grill; be careful not to overcook the scallops or they will become chewy.

- Serve immediately as a canape with drinks.

Thyme

When to plant? Hot humid climate Year-round **Hot dry climate** August–March
Cool temperate climate September–February
Seed or seedling? Seedling.
I like . . . full sun and well-draining soil.
I don't like . . . not much, pretty low-maintenance.
Feed me . . . only occasionally, with a slow-release fertiliser.
Give me a drink . . . regularly, but will cope well with dry spells.
Pick me . . . as required. Trim back after flowering to encourage bushy growth.

ROSEMARY SUNSEEKER

Rosemary thrives in warm, dry Mediterranean conditions, but it's on nippy autumn days that I'm inspired to cook with it, in slow-cooked roasts, in marinades and in homemade breads (like my Rosemary Country Bread Rolls pictured opposite, see page 113 for recipe). I love the earthiness of rosemary and the beautiful lilac flowers it sends out in early summer. It's quite astringent, so always remember to use it sparingly.

My rosemary is a prostrate variety which sends out long, drooping branches. It sits happily in the direct sun, needing only the occasional water and a prune once a year in early spring to encourage new growth. It seems to survive all manner of abuses. It could be a good one for the novice gardener.

Rosemary

When to plant? Hot humid climate Year-round **Hot dry climate** July–March
Cool temperate climate August–February
Seed or seedling? Seed or from cuttings.
I like . . . full or partial sun and well-draining soil.
I don't like . . . being overfed.
Feed me . . . twice a year with slow-release fertiliser.
Give me a drink . . . will tolerate long periods without water.
Pick me . . . as required. Regular pruning will keep shrub bushy.

Rosemary country bread rolls

Makes 12

1 × 7 g sachet dried yeast

1 cup (250 ml) warm water

1 cup (250 ml) milk

2 tablespoons sugar

½ cup (85 g) fine polenta,
plus 2 tablespoons extra

60 g unsalted butter, at
room temperature

1 small onion,
coarsely chopped

3 tablespoons coarsely
chopped rosemary, plus
extra to garnish

2 cups (320 g)
whole-wheat flour

2 cups (300 g) unbleached
self-raising flour, plus
1–1½ cups (150 g–225 g)
extra, for kneading

2 teaspoons salt

1 tablespoon freshly
ground black pepper

oil, for greasing

5 tablespoons
olive tapenade

2 tablespoons
grated parmesan

I need to knead. After a day in the office, there's nothing I enjoy more than pouring myself a glass of vino and working some dough on the benchtop. Of course, you could use the dough hook attachment on your electric mixer if you have one; just make sure you keep checking the dough with your hands so you know when you have the right consistency.

These rolls are a lovely scroll shape when cooked (pictured on page 111).

- In a large bowl, combine the yeast, warm water and milk and leave to stand for 5 minutes until the yeast has dissolved.

- Add the sugar, ½ cup polenta, butter, onion, 2 tablespoons rosemary, the whole-wheat flour, 2 cups of the self-raising flour, salt and pepper and mix well.

- Place the mixture on a lightly floured benchtop and knead for 2–3 minutes, gradually adding enough extra flour (you'll need about 1 cup) to form a workable dough. Set the dough aside covered with a clean tea towel to rest for 10–15 minutes.

- Knead the dough for a further 10 minutes until smooth and elastic, using the remaining extra flour as needed to stop it from sticking. Transfer the dough to a large lightly oiled bowl and coat with a layer of oil. Cover the bowl with a clean tea towel and set aside in a warm place for about 1½ hours or until the dough has doubled in bulk.

- When the dough has risen, knock out the air with your fist and roll out to a 2 cm-thick square. Spread with a layer of tapenade, the grated parmesan and 1 tablespoon chopped rosemary. Roll the dough up into a long log and cut into twelve equal pieces. Sprinkle a large baking tray with the extra polenta. Arrange the rolls on the tray in a round cluster, seam-side facing inwards, cover with a tea towel and set aside in a warm place for about 45 minutes or until the dough has just doubled in bulk.

- Meanwhile, preheat fan-forced oven to 175°C.

- Bake the rolls for 35–40 minutes: they should be nicely browned and sound hollow when the base is tapped with your finger. Remove the rolls from the tray, sprinkle with rosemary and cool on a wire rack. Break them into individual rolls to serve.

Roast pork with rosemary

What isn't there to love about this recipe? The pork crackling crisps up into shards of fatty caramel and the juices it releases baste the loin beneath. When it comes to pork crackling, just a little satisfies any guilty craving.

The earthiness of fresh rosemary combines so beautifully with most meats, but especially with pork. I serve this with baked vegies or, if the weather is warmer, with a bitter leaf salad or as a (very) indulgent sandwich filling.

Serves 8

1.5 kg pork loin, preferably free-range, French-trimmed

olive oil, for rubbing

⅔ cup rosemary

4 cloves organic garlic

2 tablespoons fennel seeds

2 tablespoons salt

- Preheat fan-forced oven to 200°C.

- Score the pork by carefully cutting into the outer layer of skin with a very sharp knife or a stanley knife. You could also ask your butcher to do this for you. Rub the pork all over with olive oil.

- Using a mortar and pestle, pound the rosemary, garlic, fennel seeds and salt to form a thick paste. Rub this into the pork well, making sure to fill all the cracks.

- Roast for 1½ hours, basting the pork from time to time, then reduce the oven temperature to 180°C fan-forced and roast for a further 30 minutes.

- Serve hot or at room temperature.

A FAMILY FAVOURITE

Coriander is the herb of my childhood. In all its forms, it's an essential ingredient in South African–Indian cooking: the fresh leaves, the roots and the dried seeds (whole or ground to a powder). As kids, our job was to scamper down to the veggie patch just before dinner to pick a bunch of fresh young coriander shoots. The soft musty leaves were the garnish for every home-cooked meal.

Coriander is a notoriously fussy grower, but once you come to understand its likes and dis-likes, you'll be able to enjoy it from your balcony for most of the year. The key is to continually sow seeds throughout the cooler, milder months, which will ensure a continuous supply before it bolts and goes to seed in the warmer weather. If your crop does go to seed, don't despair. The seeds are intensely fragrant and can be dried and used in your cooking, or re-sown for a new crop.

Coriander

When to plant? Hot humid climate March–September Hot dry climate March–September Cool temperate climate September–April

Seed or seedling? Seed.

I like . . . partial shade or full sun in well-draining soil.

I don't like . . . hot weather as it may cause 'bolting' (developing flowers and going to seed quickly).

Feed me . . . fortnightly with a nitrogen-rich fertiliser.

Give me a drink . . . regularly to encourage more leaf growth.

Pick me . . . harvest leaves, stalks and roots often and sow seeds every few weeks.

Thai chicken salad with chilli, spring onions and coriander

Serves 4

2 skinless chicken breast fillets (about 300 g)

2 cups (500 ml) coconut milk

1 teaspoon ground turmeric

½ teaspoon salt

3 tablespoons fish sauce

1 tablespoon lime juice

1½ teaspoons chilli powder

1½ teaspoons palm sugar

1 stalk lemongrass, finely chopped

4 red shallots, finely sliced

2 spring onions, green and white parts finely chopped

15 mint leaves, plus extra to serve

1 cup coriander leaves

banana leaves, to serve (optional)

fresh chillies, cut in half lengthways, to serve (optional)

No-one enjoys those 24-hour, long-haul flights to Europe in cattle class. To make the trip more bearable, I try to schedule an overnight stopover in Bangkok so I can refresh, soak up some tropical sun and tuck into the local street food. This refreshing Thai salad, pictured opposite, showcases what I love most about simple Thai cooking – crunchy vegetables, zingy herbs and a dressing with a perfectly balanced combination of sweet, hot, salty tang.

This recipe is similar to the one taught to me by my dear friend and chef Kham Signavong, who owns the Arun Thai restaurant in Potts Point, Sydney.

- Place the chicken breast fillets in a large heavy-based saucepan. Pour in the coconut milk to cover and add the turmeric. Bring to the boil over medium heat, then reduce the heat to low and simmer for about 15 minutes or until the chicken is cooked. Remove the chicken with a slotted spoon and transfer to a bowl to cool. Once cool enough to handle, tear the chicken into shreds with your fingers then sprinkle over salt to taste.

- In a small bowl, mix the fish sauce, lime juice, chilli powder and palm sugar together to make a dressing. In another bowl, mix the chicken with the lemongrass, shallots, spring onion, mint leaves and coriander. Pour the dressing over and combine until the chicken is well coated with the dressing.

- To serve, line bowls with banana leaves if using and spoon in the salad. Garnish with a split red chilli, if using, and some extra mint leaves.

Potato, pea and coriander samosas

Makes 60

2 tablespoons ghee

1 large brown onion, finely chopped

2 cloves organic garlic, crushed

½ teaspoon grated ginger

1 tablespoon chopped coriander root

1 teaspoon black mustard seeds

½ teaspoon ground cumin

½ teaspoon ground coriander

½ teaspoon ground fennel

½ teaspoon ground turmeric

½ teaspoon chilli powder

500 g desiree potatoes, cut into 2 cm cubes

2 teaspoons salt

½ cup (60 g) frozen peas

4 spring onions, green and white parts finely chopped

large handful coriander leaves, roughly chopped, plus extra to garnish

1 × 250 g packet spring-roll pastry (about 20 sheets), thawed if frozen

1 teaspoon self-raising flour

vegetable oil, for deep-frying

Samosas are the Indian equivalent of a meat pie, and no-one can make them as well as my sister Manika. This recipe makes about sixty samosas. After I've assembled them I usually freeze half of them in snap-lock bags to cook another time. When unexpected guests pop round, I just take the samosas straight from the freezer and drop them into gently bubbling hot oil – they're ready in no time.

- Melt the ghee in a deep frying pan or large saucepan then add the onion and cook over low heat for 10 minutes until soft and translucent. Add the garlic, ginger and coriander and cook until fragrant. Add the mustard seeds and cook until they pop, then stir in the remaining spices – be careful not to let them burn.

- Next, add the potato and toss until well coated. Season with salt, then add ¾ cup water and cook, covered, for 10–15 minutes until the potato is tender but still holding its shape. Add the peas and cook for 5 minutes. Remove the pan from the heat and stir in the spring onion and coriander leaves.

- Cut each spring-roll pastry sheet into three equal strips and cover with a damp tea towel. In a small bowl, mix the flour with 2 teaspoons water to form a thick paste.

- Take one rectangular strip of pastry and place the bottom edge on your palm. Fold the bottom left edge of pastry over to the right side of the pastry strip. Now take the bottom right edge and fold it to the left side to form a triangular cone. (If you're finding this tricky to do in your hand, just place the pastry on your benchtop.) Take the cone in your hand and open it out to form a cavity. Place a heaped dessertspoon of the potato filling in the cone then fold the pastry across to form a triangle (take care not to overfill the samosa). Keep folding until you reach the end of the strip, then wet the edges with a little paste and press down firmly to seal. Make sure there are no holes or exposed bits of filling. Repeat with the remaining pastry strips and filling to make sixty samosas.

- Pour the oil into a frying pan to a depth of about 5 cm and heat over low–medium heat. Cook the samosas in batches, taking care not to crowd the pan, until they are lightly golden. Remove with a slotted spoon and drain on paper towel.

- Garnish with coriander and serve with some cucumber and mint raita alongside if you like.

Garlic

When to plant? Hot humid climate March–July **Hot dry climate** April–August
Cool temperate climate March–September

Seed or seedling? Plant garlic cloves from a nursery or specialist grower.

I like . . . full sun and loose, well-draining soil.

I don't like . . . hot, humid weather.

Feed me . . . liquid fertiliser after shoots appear.

Give me a drink . . . frequently, especially during hot weather.

Pick me . . . after 6–8 months; dig up bulbs when leaves turn yellow. Hang to dry in a cool, dark spot in the kitchen.

GARLIC – SORTS OUT WHO YOUR FRIENDS ARE

Being able to grow my own garlic is a real thrill. I use garlic in nearly every dish I cook from every cuisine, including Italian, Greek, Thai, Indian and Moroccan. It's an essential base ingredient and a natural fortifying antibiotic. My friends don't seem to mind my excessive consumption – well, the ones that still speak to me, that is.

Garlic was one of those vegetables I couldn't imagine would be possible to grow on a balcony. I don't know why, but I automatically put it in the fantasy vegetable category – too exotic and high-maintenance to ever adapt to the vagaries of balcony life. In fact, as I discovered after a bit of research, garlic is actually a very easy crop to grow, although with a six–eight month growing season, it takes delayed gratification to a whole new level. The best time to plant garlic is a month or so before the cold weather really sets in, usually around late June (although I planted my cloves in early June as it was already cool enough). The garlic can then be harvested when the leaves die back around mid-December. This gives the plant time to grow large, strong bulbs.

Well, here goes. I'm planting my first crop of organic cloves from a Tasmanian mail-order nursery in a recycled plastic planter bag with several holes in the bottom. The purplish-pink papery cloves will be buried in rich organic compost and lovingly watered and fertilised. I've also thrown in some special manure from 'Gundooee', a cattle property near Mudgee in New South Wales run by my good mates Rob and Nita Lennon. It's been produced by some very happy wagyu/angus-cross cows and should make the garlic extra flavoursome. Anyway, I'm sure that whatever I get will be a vast improvement on the insipid bleached bulbs from China that fill our grocery shelves.

BEWITCHING BORAGE

Unexpectedly, my greatest autumn joy has come from the borage bushes I planted from seed in hanging baskets back in late January. They are deep-rooted with long, robust stems and the most beautiful delicate five-pointed mauve flowers I've ever seen. And best of all, they don't seem to require any special attention.

Borage is an old-fashioned plant that most of us associate with traditional English cottage gardens. I wanted to grow it for several reasons. Firstly, borage is a wonderful attractant to bees, and when you live 40 metres up in the air surrounded by concrete and glass, believe me, it's difficult to get bees to drop in. Sure enough, within a day of the first buds flowering, I had several bees buzzing around the borage for a sip of nectar while, at the same time, doing some important pollinating for me.

Secondly, both the stems and the flowers of the borage plant are edible. The soft-haired stems can be stir-fried like you would asparagus or beans, and the delicate flowers have a wonderful sugary taste that complements desserts and cakes. Truth be told, I find my borage flowers too beautiful to eat. I just love watching the early-morning autumn sun shine through their translucent petals, creating little mauve stained-glass windows. Pure, unadulterated joy.

Borage

When to plant? Hot humid climate Year-round Hot dry climate Year-round Cool temperate climate October–February

Seed or seedling? Seed.

I like . . . moist, loose soil.

I don't like . . . frosts or high winds; aphids.

Feed me . . . once a month with liquid fertiliser (can grow up to 1 metre tall).

Give me a drink . . . regularly.

Pick me . . . as soon as flowers emerge.

Stephanie's pavlova with fresh cream and borage flowers

This pavlova recipe from the first edition of Stephanie Alexander's *The Cook's Companion* is a favourite of mine. I omit the passionfruit and use edible flowers instead – it's a great showcase for my harvest of beautiful lilac-coloured borage. Borage flowers are very sweet and often used in desserts and cake-making.

Serves 12

4 organic egg whites, at room temperature

pinch of salt

250 g caster sugar

1 tablespoon cornflour

1 teaspoon white-wine vinegar

few drops of vanilla extract

300 ml thickened cream, firmly whipped

borage flowers, for decorating

- Preheat fan-forced oven to 170°C. Line a baking tray with baking paper and draw on a 20 cm circle.

- Beat the egg whites and salt together until soft satiny peaks form. Beat in the sugar, a little at a time, until incorporated and the texture is smooth. Gently fold in the corn-flour, vinegar and vanilla, then heap the mixture into one even mound within the outline of your circle. Flatten the top and smooth the edges with a spatula.

- Place in the oven, immediately reduce the temperature to 150°C fan-forced and cook for 1 hour. Turn off the oven and leave the meringue in there to cool and dry out completely, for a few hours or preferably overnight.

- To serve, place the meringue on a stand or platter and cover with the whipped cream, then scatter over the borage flowers.

MUSHROOMS

SORREL

WARRIGAL GRE̶E̶N̶S̶

RADISH

STRAWBERRIES
ROCKET

CURRY LEAF

ALFALFA SPROUTS

OREGANO

WINTER

Temperatures are plunging and the winds are whipping up.
The plants seem to instinctively know it's do-or-die time
out there. They try to hunker down, but on a high-rise
balcony there is no place to hide.

WINTER WONDERLAND

How plants have adapted to winter with its frosts, rain and icy winds is quite simply a miracle to me. Unlike us, most plants have to stay outdoors exposed to the harsh elements. They either adapt or perish.

Of course, I'm discovering that some plants are better at this than others. Green leafy vegetables thrive in these bracing conditions, as do root vegetables which can burrow deep into the soil where temperatures are more forgiving. Well, that's in a regular garden. When you're on the edge of a blustery thirteenth-floor balcony, survival, even for the winter-hardy, becomes that much dicier.

Winter has brought with it an unsettling realisation. I'm beginning to feel a little disengaged and disconnected from my plants. I'm not as involved. Perhaps it's because there's not much growing going on. The little action that is happening is hidden underground. It looks so bare and bleak out there. Am I sending my winter crops to an almost certain death? Or will they rise to the challenge?

Mark must sense my melancholy. He's been unusually supportive and encouraging of late. Or is it just a reverse-psychology ruse? If all the plants wither away he'll get his balcony back, I suppose. I can never tell with him.

It's too late to turn back though. My 'sacrificial lambs' have been chosen: mushrooms, curry leaves, rocket, warrigal greens, sorrel, radishes, alfalfa and oregano – an intriguing mix of native, French and Italian varieties. And, to give me something tantalisingly delicious to look forward to, I'm potting two varieties of strawberries as well. Who will get to taste them first? Me or the voracious slugs?

Mushrooms

When to plant? Hot humid climate June–August **Hot dry climate** March–November **Cool temperate climate** February–December

Seed or seedling? Mushroom kits already impregnated with spores can be purchased during winter.

I like . . . moist, dark conditions.

I don't like . . . light.

Feed me . . . kits contain necessary nutrients in the growing medium.

Give me a drink . . . spray with water every day.

Pick me . . . as mushrooms appear. Gently twist at the base to remove.

ALWAYS ROOM FOR SOME MUSHIES

Mushrooms have been one of my favourite vegetables (although technically a fungi) since I was a child. One of my many gardening chores was picking mushrooms from the big mushroom compost sack my parents kept in our tool shed. It was damp, dark and cold in there: perfect conditions for growing mushrooms.

These days you can buy mushroom-growing kits which have been inoculated with mushroom spores and will last for one 2–3 week growing season. But, a warning – the first mushroom kit I bought from a popular hardware chain turned mouldy and bore no mushrooms. My hours of pampering had been for nothing. So purchase only reputable kits from trusted suppliers (I used *fungi.net.au*).

You can buy mushroom kits for many varieties of mushroom, from regular white button mushrooms to enoki, oyster or swiss brown, which I grew. When your kit arrives in the mail, all you need to do is mix the mushroom compost with the inoculated casings and dampen the contents with a daily spray of water. Keep the box in a cool, dark place such as a cupboard or in the garage. My north-facing balcony is flooded with winter sun, so I made a home for my mushrooms in the laundry, on top of the washing machine (as you do).

The mushrooms will begin to emerge within two or three weeks and all you need to do to harvest them is twist them at their base and pull gently. The longer you leave them, the larger and deeper-flavoured they will become. Your little edible pincushions should keep emerging for at least a month until the spores have depleted their food source. After you've picked your mushrooms, rub them with a cloth to remove any grit. Don't run them under water or they'll get spongy and lose their flavour.

My home-grown mushrooms were extra-ordinarily crunchy and nothing like their mushy supermarket cousins. Breakfast has been a simple case of throwing some sliced mushrooms into a pan with some frothing butter, garlic and parsley and spooning them onto some thick toast. How easy and nutritious is that? It's also a very effective bribe for an old-fashioned husband who thinks laundries should be used for washing clothes.

Buttered mushrooms on toast

**Mushrooms on toast, served in bed with the papers on a lazy weekend –
no need to say more. For an extra bit of indulgence, use a rich cultured butter
to complement the earthy flavours of your mushrooms. And watch
out for toast crumbs between the sheets . . .**

Serves 2

40 g cultured (or European-style) butter

500 g swiss brown, button or portobello
mushrooms, chopped into bite-sized pieces

2 cloves organic garlic, finely sliced

salt and freshly ground black pepper

squeeze of fresh lemon juice

small handful flat-leaf parsley leaves, finely chopped

2 slices toasted sourdough, to serve

- Melt the butter in a large heavy-based frying pan over medium heat until foaming, then add the mushrooms, garlic and a little salt and pepper and fry for about 5 minutes or until the water has evaporated from the mushrooms and they are beginning to colour.

- Remove the pan from the heat and stir through the lemon juice and parsley, then serve immediately on toasted sourdough.

Chicken and mushroom pot pies

My elderly mother-in-law, Gwendolyn, loves these pot pies and can wolf down a couple in one sitting. They are the ultimate comfort food – crisp, flaky pastry with a creamy chicken and mushroom filling.

You'll need eight 10 cm ramekins for this recipe.

Makes 8

1 roasted or barbecued chicken, meat shredded

1 cup chopped chives

⅓ cup chopped tarragon

10 swiss brown mushrooms, quartered

1½ cups (360 g) sour cream

½ cup (125 ml) chicken stock

sea salt and white pepper

2 sheets ready-rolled puff pastry, thawed if frozen

1 organic egg, beaten

green salad, to serve

- Preheat fan-forced oven to 200°C.

- In a large bowl, mix together the chicken, herbs, mushrooms, sour cream, chicken stock and salt and pepper to taste.

- Lay the pastry sheets out on a clean benchtop and cut eight rounds of pastry slightly larger than your ramekins. Fill the ramekins with the chicken mixture and top with a pastry lid, then brush with beaten egg. Press down the edges to seal and sprinkle with salt.

- Bake on an oven tray for 20 minutes until the pastry is puffed and golden, then serve with a leafy green salad.

Mushroom and spinach frittata

Serves 4

1 bunch spinach, washed
and trimmed

30 g butter

⅓ cup thinly sliced
golden shallots

300 g swiss brown
mushrooms, sliced

6 organic eggs

¼ cup (50 g) goat's
cheese, crumbled

¼ cup (20 g)
grated parmesan

handful flat-leaf parsley
leaves, coarsely chopped

rocket salad, to serve

Confit tomato

200 g very ripe tomatoes,
preferably roma

1 cup (250 ml) light olive oil

1 clove organic
garlic, halved

pinch of crushed
white peppercorns

1 sprig thyme

1 bay leaf

You can't make a tasty frittata without good eggs, but finding fresh eggs laid by happy hens isn't always easy. Australia's labelling laws mean even chickens that spend most of their day indoors in a barn can be classed as 'free-range'. The best option is to buy eggs that are certified organic, or to buy them from small delis or farmers' markets.

- To make the confit tomato, first blanch the tomatoes to make them easier to peel. With a sharp knife score the top of the tomatoes with a small cross, being careful not to cut too deep. Bring a large saucepan of water to the boil, carefully place in the tomatoes and remove the pan from the heat. Leave for about 30 seconds then remove the tomatoes with a slotted spoon and place in a colander. Peel each tomato and discard the skin. Chop the flesh into quarters and remove the seeds.

- Heat the oil in a large heavy-based saucepan over low heat. Just before it begins to simmer add the tomatoes, garlic, white pepper and herbs. Cook for 10–15 minutes until the tomatoes are just tender but not soft, then remove from the heat and leave the tomatoes to cool in the pan. Once cool, scoop five tomato quarters out and set aside, and transfer the remaining tomatoes, oil and seasonings to a jar or an airtight container. They will keep in the fridge for up to 2 weeks.

- Meanwhile, bring a large saucepan of water to the boil, carefully place in the spinach leaves and remove the pan from the heat. Leave for 1 minute, then refresh in iced water. Drain, squeeze out any excess water and chop the leaves finely, then set aside.

- Melt the butter in a heavy-based ovenproof frying pan over medium–high heat until foaming. Add the shallots and mushrooms and cook for about 10 minutes or until soft.

- Meanwhile, lightly beat the eggs in a bowl and stir through the cheeses and parsley. Preheat your grill to medium.

- Add the cooked spinach and tomato to the mushroom mixture, reduce the heat to low and heat through for a couple of minutes. Pour over the egg mixture, lightly fork it through and cook over medium heat for 2–3 minutes until the egg is just beginning to set. Transfer the frying pan to the preheated grill and cook for 5–8 minutes or until the frittata is cooked through.

- Cut into wedges and serve with a rocket salad.

WHAT'S UP, DOC?

It's been three months since I planted my carrot seeds, and they're finally ready to harvest. Orange-coloured carrots are so ubiquitous that it's easy to forget carrots come in many hues – from purple to red to cream. In fact, the first carrots are thought to have been small, purple and woody and to have originated in Afghanistan. It was a clever band of Dutch farmers in the eighteenth century who – using seed selection – popularised the large orange variety we know today as The Carrot. I could only find seed for the orange variety so that's what I grew.

Pulling my first carrot crop from its pot was quite a surreal experience. There I was, thirteen floors up in the air, with skyscrapers in the background, holding a 3-kilo bunch of fat orange fingers that emerged covered in dirt: it doesn't come any fresher. Just call me Farmer Naidoo. My confidence was soaring; I was having delusions of grandeur. Maybe a balcony chicken run wasn't such an impossibility after all, or perhaps that water buffalo for some milky mozzarella . . .

Carrots

When to plant? Hot humid climate February–November Hot dry climate July–March Cool temperate climate September–February

Seed or seedling? Will grow much better from seed than seedlings. Carrot seeds are tiny so will need thinning out as they mature.

I like . . . rich, well-draining, loose soil.

I don't like . . . fertilisers that are high in nitrogen.

Feed me . . . liquid fertiliser fortnightly, but don't overfeed.

Give me a drink . . . regularly, especially during dry spells.

Pick me . . . 12–16 weeks after planting.

Fitz's carrot salsa

**My husband, Mark, is a salad freak. He has to have a salad
every day otherwise he goes into meltdown. He makes a large bowl
of this carrot salsa to have with curries (like Selvie's Chicken Curry with
Curry Leaves on page 154), grilled steak or just on its own. Mark says
a good salsa is all about good ingredients; the best extra virgin olive oil
you can get, the freshest herbs, and the best-quality organic vegetables.
Fortunately my balcony carrots made the grade.**

Serves 4 as a side salad

2 carrots, grated

1 cup (80 g) shredded red cabbage

½ green capsicum (pepper), seeds and white membrane removed, flesh chopped

½ cup finely chopped flat-leaf parsley

2 tablespoons olive oil

2 tablespoons red-wine vinegar

salt and freshly ground black pepper

- Combine the carrot, red cabbage, capsicum and parsley in a bowl and toss well.
- Whisk together the oil and vinegar and stir through the salad. Season to taste and serve.

Carrot cake with cream-cheese icing

Serves 10

4 organic eggs

250 g soft brown sugar

¾ cup (180 ml) vegetable oil

2½ cups (375 g) plain flour

1 teaspoon salt

2 teaspoons baking powder

1 teaspoon bicarbonate
of soda

2 teaspoons cinnamon

1 teaspoon
ground cardamom

8 medium-sized carrots
(about 400 g), grated

½ cup chopped pecans

Cream-cheese icing

180 g butter,
at room temperature

250 g icing sugar

180 g cream cheese

3 drops vanilla extract

1 tablespoon lemon juice

My sisters Suraya and Manika and I spent quite a bit of our childhoods living in small regional towns in Tasmania and South Australia. Carrot cake always reminds us of those particularly 'country' experiences – fairs, fetes, raffles, knitted tea-cosies and country bake-offs. This carrot cake is light and very moist. Try stopping at one slice.

- Preheat fan-forced oven to 180°C and grease and flour a 24 cm springform cake pan.

- In an electric mixer, beat the eggs and sugar until pale and creamy, then beat in the oil.

- In a separate bowl, sift the flour, salt, baking powder, bicarbonate of soda, cinnamon and cardamom. Add the egg mixture and stir to incorporate well. Add the grated carrot and pecans and fold through gently.

- Pour the batter into the prepared tin and bake for 1 hour or until a skewer inserted into the middle of the cake comes out clean. Leave to cool for a few minutes in the tin and then turn out onto a wire rack to cool completely.

- When cooled, carefully slice the cake lengthways into two even discs.

- To make the icing, combine the butter and sugar, then add the cream cheese and whip until stiff and fluffy. Add the vanilla and lemon juice and combine.

- Spread a thick layer of icing over one disc, then sandwich the other disc on top. Spread the remaining icing on top.

FINALLY GROWING UP

Back in summer, I went all hi-tech and had a vertical green wall unit installed on my balcony. We balcony gardeners need to be smart about how to maximise space, and vertical gardening is a very clever solution. There are options for every budget; from simple, cheap wooden trellises with hooks for pots to the space-age all-in-one unit that I was lucky enough to trial. The ecoVert vertical wall unit is a clever prototype that's not yet commercially available. It's made from lightweight recycled plastic and developed by Sydney company, Junglefy. It consists of a bracket attached to the wall, and two pods with holes which hold the plants in pockets in a light soil medium made from potting mix, manure, the mineral perlite and coconut fibre. The plants are watered by hand through an opening at the top of the unit and an electric pump drives the water from the reservoir around the unit. It's expected to retail for about $400 when it completes its trial phase.

I planted ten seedlings, making sure to leave an empty pocket between each so the plants had room to expand. I selected a mix of herbs, greens and bug-repelling plants – warrigal greens, sorrel, Vietnamese mint, oregano, thyme, common mint, feverfew, coral lettuce, butter lettuce and chives. The lack of sun on that wall during summer wasn't good for the delicate seedlings, and the strong winds that whipped up in late February really gave them a battering. White bugs attacked and killed off the oregano, common mint and some lettuces, leaving only the warrigal greens, sorrel, feverfew and Vietnamese mint clinging to life. They've certainly earned their own reality TV show: *Survivor – Potts Point*.

My balcony is now awash with northerly winter sun. The survivors are cascading from their little wall pockets, creating a wondrous living edible wall sculpture. (Actually, the feverfew is the only plant on my balcony that isn't edible. Its role is as an aphid and mealy-bug repellent. Despite its pretty, daisy-like white petals with yellow centres, it emits a strong odour that bad bugs find offensive; a 24-hour sentinel that makes my bug patrols much easier.)

I've found that vertical walls are ideal for shallow-rooted greens, herbs, and plants such as warrigal greens and Vietnamese mint which need plenty of space to ramble.

Just like on-the-ground balcony plants though, your vertical plants still need at least four–six hours of sunlight a day, a regular watering and an occasional fertiliser feed, and they are especially vulnerable to strong winds. My biggest mistake was planting edibles with invasive roots at the top of the green wall rather than at the bottom. The warrigal greens and the sorrel now suck up most of the water as it filters down through the unit, cutting off supplies to plants further down. You live and learn, I guess.

Warrigal greens are a crunchier, more robust version of spinach that grow wild along most of Australia's tropical eastern seaboard. I've been bewitched by them ever since first trying them in a family-run Italian restaurant in South West Rocks on the New South Wales north coast. Even though they're native, you rarely find them in stores or at the markets, so growing my own stash was the best option. Sorrel has soft, billowing leaves and its tangy lemony flavour makes it a wonderful addition to a sauce for fish or as the star ingredient, blanched and blitzed into a soup. These two plants need plenty of room to ramble and a vertical wall is just the spot. A note of caution here: sorrel, warrigal greens, spinach and many other leafy greens and vegetables contain significant quantities of oxalates. Oxalates are naturally occurring plant compounds which can be harmful when consumed in excessive amounts. Blanching your greens reduces the level of oxalates significantly because the water absorbs some of the oxalate; other forms of cooking have less impact on diminishing the oxalate level. However, there is no need to be

alarmed about your intake of oxalates if you are consuming small quantities of these greens: the nutritional benefits from consuming greens far outweigh the risks.

The other success on the wall has been the Vietnamese mint, which curls and twists its stems in big arcs. Vietnamese mint is actually not a true mint and is sometimes called Vietnamese coriander as well. It's probably called mint because it exhibits similar qualities – it thrives in wet conditions and grows without much attention. It's an essential ingredient in Asian salads, soups, rice paper rolls and stir-fries, imparting a warm tangy pungency to dishes.

And the feverfew, while doing a good job warding off bad bugs, is becoming a pest itself. I need to hack it back every few weeks so it doesn't bush up too much and block the light from the other vertical edibles.

Sorrel

When to plant? Hot humid climate Year-round Hot dry climate Year-round
Cool temperate climate Year-round

Seed or seedling? Seed.

I like . . . full sun or semi-shade.

I don't like . . . frosts; aphids, snails and slugs.

Feed me . . . half the recommended dose of liquid fertiliser every month.

Give me a drink . . . frequently during warm weather.

Pick me . . . regularly.

Warrigal greens

When to plant? Hot humid climate September–November Hot dry climate
December–February Cool temperate climate Not suitable

Seed or seedling? Seeds germinate slowly, or you can propagate from cuttings.

I like . . . warm, moist air.

I don't like . . . frosts.

Feed me . . . once a month with liquid fertiliser.

Give me a drink . . . often, will need plenty of water.

Pick me . . . leaves can be picked as they mature but they must be blanched before use to remove harmful oxalates.

MADAME LASH PAYS A VISIT

It's blowing a gale out there. Antarctic winds are hooning through Potts Point like Formula One cars. The plants on the balcony seem to be in a Broadway chorus line choreographed by a hyper Bob Fosse: their tiny stems and shoots contort and snap back and forth in time to a silent score. One moment they are in tranquil repose, the next they are in violent convulsions. I feel helpless. I've managed to move some of the plants off the exposed railing to a more sheltered position against the wall, but the rest are just going to have to fend for themselves. I say a little prayer.

The next morning, I open the curtains with a heavy heart. It will be carnage out there after those winds. How could anything have survived? But the damage is not as severe as I had feared. Debris and dust are scattered across the balcony, leaves have been battered and bruised, flower buds have been crushed. A few stalks have snapped and lie scattered across the tiled floor. I pull on my gloves, grab a bag and start picking up body parts. Some of the yields from the radishes and carrots and the edible greens on the wall will be down, but I count myself lucky. I give the dehydrated plants a deep watering in the hope they'll bounce back with few scars.

Pan-fried salmon with sorrel butter

Herbed butters are a quick way to add flavour to fish, grilled meats, vegetables or breads. I try to make double the quantity of this sorrel butter and freeze half into discs that I can use to lift a mid-week dinner.

Consumption of fish reached record levels in 2010, decimating the world's fish stocks. When buying seafood, always look for the Marine Stewardship Council label as this denotes a sustainable fish variety.

Serves 4

100 g butter

4 salmon fillets

salt and freshly ground black pepper

Sorrel butter

200 g softened butter, coarsely chopped

3 handfuls sorrel leaves

2 golden shallots, finely chopped

1 tablespoon red-wine vinegar

salt and freshly ground black pepper

- To make the sorrel butter, blend all the ingredients in a food processor until well combined. Season to taste, wrap tightly with plastic film to form a log and chill in the fridge for 20 minutes.

- Heat the 100 g butter in a large heavy-based pan. Add the salmon fillets, skin-side down, and cook for 5–6 minutes or until the skin is crisp. Turn the fish, season well and cook for 1–2 minutes to colour the other side.

- Serve each salmon fillet with a disc of sorrel butter on top.

Sorrel soup with mascarpone

Sorrel adds a lovely lemony flavour to dishes. You can eat the young leaves raw in salads, but the older leaves should be cooked. Add them at the last moment to soups and casseroles to retain their colour and flavour.

Serves 4

4 handfuls sorrel

25 g unsalted butter

1 small onion, finely chopped

1 leek, finely chopped

1 potato, finely chopped

1 teaspoon salt

55 g mascarpone, plus extra to serve

freshly ground black pepper

½ cup (40 g) freshly grated parmesan

2 slices bread

1 clove organic garlic, halved

olive oil, for drizzling

- Wash the sorrel thoroughly and remove any fibrous stalks, then roughly chop.

- Melt the butter in a deep heavy-based saucepan over medium heat, then fry the onion, leek and potato for about 5 minutes or until the onion and leek are soft. Pour in 1 litre water to cover the vegetables, add the salt, bring to the boil and cook for 8 minutes. Add the sorrel, reduce the heat to low–medium and simmer for 2–3 minutes. Remove from the heat and leave to cool a little, then puree to a thick soup with a stick blender. Stir through the mascarpone, season to taste and top with grated parmesan.

- Meanwhile, toast two pieces of bread and, while still hot, rub one side of each slice with a halved clove of garlic. Drizzle with olive oil.

- Serve the soup warm with an extra dollop of mascarpone swirled in, accompanied by garlic bruschetta.

Warrigal greens with walnut crumbs and parmesan crisps

Serves 4 as a side

1 cup (80 g)
grated parmesan

6 handfuls warrigal greens

½ cup (50 g) walnuts

20 g butter

1 tablespoon olive oil, plus
extra for drizzling

2 cloves organic
garlic, sliced

sea salt and freshly
ground Tasmanian
mountain pepper

Australia is so rich in bush foods that we really should incorporate more into our cooking. Native species have adapted to our nutrient-depleted soils and our drought conditions, so it makes good environmental sense to use them. A whole array of ingredients, such as the Tasmanian mountain pepper used here, are now available. Try Sydney company A Taste of the Bush (see *atasteofthebush.com.au* for stockists in your state).

You can substitute baby spinach leaves and regular black pepper if you can't get your hands on any warrigal greens or native pepper.

- To make the parmesan crisps, preheat fan-forced oven to 200°C and grease and line a large baking tray.

- Place an egg ring on the prepared tray and fill to the top with grated cheese. Carefully lift the egg ring off, leaving a disc of cheese. Repeat until you've used up all the cheese, leaving about 2 cm between each disc. Bake for 10 minutes until golden and crisp then remove from the oven and set aside.

- Blanch the warrigal greens in just-boiled water for 2 minutes, then refresh in iced water and drain well. Chop roughly and set aside.

- Dry-fry the walnuts over low heat in a small frying pan until just toasted. Allow to cool slightly and chop finely.

- Melt the butter and oil in a large heavy-based pan and add the garlic, frying for 2–3 minutes until fragrant. Add the blanched warrigal greens and heat through, then add salt and pepper to taste.

- Serve the greens sprinkled with walnut crumbs. Drizzle over some extra olive oil and top with a parmesan crisp.

Twice-baked cheese souffles with a blue cheese and warrigal greens cream

Makes 6

90 g butter, chopped

⅓ cup (50 g) self-raising flour

1 cup (250 ml) milk

3 large organic eggs, separated

125 g gruyere, coarsely grated

1 clove organic garlic, crushed

½ teaspoon olive oil

3 handfuls warrigal greens, cut into fine strips, plus extra leaves to garnish

3 cups (750 ml) boiling water

Blue cheese and warrigal greens cream

1 cup (250 ml) thickened cream

125 g mascarpone

125 g good-quality blue cheese or other strongly flavoured cheese, crumbled

2 handfuls warrigal greens, shredded

salt and freshly ground black pepper

Say the word souffle and I usually run for cover. Twice-baked souffles, however, remove all those 'will it rise or won't it?' paranoias. You can do the first bake the day before, pop them in the fridge and finish them off the next day. Too easy.

The warrigal greens in this recipe can be replaced with baby spinach leaves for an equally delicious result.

- Preheat fan-forced oven to 180°C and lightly grease six ½ cup (125 ml) capacity ramekins.

- Melt the butter over medium heat in a large heavy-based saucepan, then add the flour and stir for 1–2 minutes until the flour starts to colour. Gradually add the milk, stirring continuously, then bring to the boil and cook for 5–6 minutes until thickened. Transfer the mixture to a bowl, add the egg yolks, gruyere, garlic, oil and warrigal greens, and stir to combine.

- In a separate bowl, whisk the egg whites until soft peaks form. Gently fold one-third of the egg whites into the cheese mixture until just combined, then fold in the remaining egg whites. Divide the mixture between the prepared ramekins and place them in a baking dish. Pour in enough boiling water to come halfway up the sides of the ramekins. Place the dish in the oven and cook for 20 minutes or until the souffles are puffed, golden and slightly firm to the touch. Remove from the oven and let the souffles cool in the ramekins.

- At this point you can refrigerate the souffles in their ramekins for up to 24 hours before serving.

- When ready to cook, preheat fan-forced oven to 200°C.

- Invert the souffles onto a baking paper-lined baking tray and cook for 20 minutes or until puffed.

- Meanwhile, for the blue cheese and warrigal greens cream, heat the thickened cream over medium heat in a saucepan to just below boiling point, then add the mascarpone and blue cheese and stir continuously until just melted. Add the warrigal greens, season to taste and simmer for 1 minute.

- Transfer the souffles to individual plates, pour over the cream and serve immediately, garnishing with extra warrigal greens.

THE ABC OF 'JARDENING'

Growing sprouts is like taking candy from a baby: too easy. You don't even need a balcony. All you need is a jar, a lid with some holes in it, and some water. Just one tablespoon of seeds will fill a jar with sprouts. Keep the jar in a warm place and wash fresh water through your seeds a few times a day. Within seven to ten days, you can harvest all manner of sprouts, from radish to bean.

I get excited about alfalfa sprouts (yes, I know – I need to get out more). All sprouts are packed with nutrition but these white thread-like rascals with green tops are the only plant to provide the full range of vitamins, from A to K. Throw them into sandwiches, salads or use them as a slightly mustardy counterbalance to meats and seafood.

Alfalfa sprouts

When to plant? Hot humid climate Year-round **Hot dry climate** Year-round Cool temperate climate Year-round

Seed or seedling? Seed: 1 tablespoon of seeds will develop into 5 cm-long sprouts and fill a small jar. Keep the seed moistened in a jar with holes in the lid and regularly washed with water until germination.

I like . . . to be kept moist and warm.

I don't like . . . drying out.

Feed me . . . no need to fertilise.

Give me a drink . . . every day.

Pick me . . . after about 7 days.

Curry-leaf tree

When to plant? Hot humid climate Year-round Hot dry climate September–February Cool temperate climate Not suitable (other than in coastal locations)

Seed or seedling? Sold as potted plants in nurseries. Can grow up to 5 metres tall.

I like . . . the tropics: warm, frost-free coastal areas.

I don't like . . . frosts.

Feed me . . . slow-release liquid fertiliser every month.

Give me a drink . . . occasionally, then more regularly as weather warms.

Pick me . . . as needed. Will freeze well in plastic snap-lock bags.

WHO'S A GOOD BOY, THEN?

A mother shouldn't have favourites, but I unashamedly do. My towering curry leaf tree, nurtured back to health after a bug attack last year, has grown into a fine, strapping young specimen (it would be gargantuan by now if I didn't keep trimming back its branches). I call it my Magic Pudding, because it just keeps on giving and giving. I hardly need to do anything

to it, just give it a thorough watering every now and then, occasionally with some fish emulsion fertiliser mixed in with the water. It seems to thrive in its roomy, 1 metre-high pot in a shady position at the back of the balcony.

Its elegantly tapered leaves are pungent and aromatic. I love rubbing a few leaves between my fingers, closing my eyes and imagining I'm in Raj India surrounded by exotic fabrics and baskets of spices. I use the leaves to flavour, as the name suggests, curries and rice dishes. Hearing them pop and crackle as they release their volatile oils when dropped in melted ghee sends me straight back to my childhood.

The tree is not at its happiest in winter, given its tropical sub-continental origins, but it's in winter that I crave its flavour in rich, thick-sauced Indian curries, pilaus and dhals. When the temperature drops, curry-leaf trees yellow and shed some of their leaves. But I don't mind. It's readying itself for the first tasty new shoots of spring.

Selvie's chicken curry with curry leaves

Serves 6

2 tablespoons ghee

2 brown onions, finely sliced

4 cloves organic garlic, crushed

5 cm piece young ginger, grated

1 cinnamon stick

3 cardamom pods, cracked

4 cloves

2 dried bay leaves

20 curry leaves

2 teaspoons ground fennel

1 teaspoon ground coriander

1 teaspoon ground turmeric

1 teaspoon hot smoked paprika

1 teaspoon mild curry powder

3 teaspoons salt

6–8 chicken drumsticks

2 large tomatoes, chopped

6 potatoes, skin left on, scrubbed and halved

1.5 litres boiling water

handful chopped coriander leaves

steamed basmati rice, to serve

I know everyone thinks their mum is the best cook in the world, but my mum, Selvie, really is. It's taken me years to replicate her famed chicken curry that she learnt to cook from her mother while she was growing up in South Africa. This curry was one of our childhood favourites. I love the aromatic flavours from all the spices and the fresh curry leaves.

- Melt the ghee in a large heavy-based casserole over medium heat. Add the onion and cook for 10 minutes or until it is just beginning to caramelise. Add the garlic and ginger and cook, stirring, for 1 minute. Add the cinnamon, cardamom, cloves, bay and curry leaves and fry for 2–3 minutes or until fragrant. Reduce the heat to low, add the ground spices and salt and fry for 3–4 minutes. Be careful not to burn the spices or the curry will have an acrid taste; you may need to add a little more ghee if the mixture gets too dry.

- Increase the heat to medium–high and add the chicken pieces, turning to ensure they are well coated with the spices. Fry for 5–8 minutes or until the chicken pieces are golden. Add the chopped tomato and cook for 10 minutes until it has reduced to a thick sauce. Next add the potato and cook for 5 minutes. Finally, add the boiling water and cook over medium–high heat for about 1 hour or until the potato is soft. The liquid will have reduced by half, and the potato will have thickened the sauce slightly.

- Stir through the coriander and serve the curry with steamed basmati rice alongside.

VITAMIN BOOSTER

Toss out your multivitamin supplements and plant some radishes instead. These pint-sized bulbs pack quite a nutrient punch, and they are extremely easy to grow in pots. When they're fresh – and I'm not talking about 'supermarket' fresh, but 'fresh from the ground' fresh – they are brimming with antioxidants, vitamin C, folates, vitamin B6, riboflavin, thiamine and minerals such as iron, magnesium, copper and calcium. Like my aphids, I enjoy radishes and their tasty leaves raw, when you can really appreciate their peppery bite. Toss them through salads, grate them into salsas, or have them the way I love to, simply dipped whole into a garlic and anchovy sauce.

Radishes

When to plant? Hot humid climate Year-round Hot dry climate Year-round Cool temperate climate Year-round

Seed or seedling? Seed. Quick to crop.

I like . . . well-draining soil in a sunny or partially sunny spot.

I don't like . . . overcrowding; aphids.

Feed me . . . a non-nitrogen fertiliser once a month.

Give me a drink . . . once or twice a week, more in warm weather.

Pick me . . . in 3–6 weeks.

Radishes with warmed anchovy sauce

Italian cooking is so regional. Sometimes just by crossing a road you can step into a quite different and distinct variation of the cuisine. Northern Italian cooking from the chilly Piedmont region has become a favourite of mine. The area is famous for its white truffles, big-flavoured Barolo wines and bagna cauda sauce, made with anchovies and garlic and usually served hot with raw vegetables. (Hot and raw is a wonderful combination if you've never tried it before.)

**This anchovy sauce is a variation of bagna cauda.
If you don't have radishes at hand, try it with celery, carrots, fennel,
green beans or even pieces of cooked potato.**

Serves 4

12 good-quality anchovy fillets

2 cloves organic garlic

1 cup (250 ml) olive oil

salt and freshly ground black pepper

1 bunch radishes, with leaves attached

- Using a mortar and pestle, crush the anchovies and garlic into a rough paste.

- Transfer the paste to a small saucepan, whisk in the olive oil until blended, then heat over very low heat until the sauce is just warm.

- Season with salt and pepper, and serve in a small dish with the radishes alongside.

NO WEED HAS EVER TASTED THIS GOOD

I didn't taste rocket until I was well into my twenties. Suddenly it was on every restaurant menu, replacing the apparently very unfashionable iceberg lettuce. We've all lost count of the number of times we've had a rocket and parmesan salad. It wasn't until my first trip to Italy that I discovered that rocket has been cultivated for centuries there and grows like a weed on the side of the road and between train tracks.

Rocket is a member of the *brassica* genus and hence loves the cold. Pick the leaves from the outside as they develop, and pinch off any flowers you see to prolong leaf growth. And don't just have rocket in salads. Try stirring it through hot pasta or stir-frying it with some onion and garlic.

Rocket

When to plant? Hot humid climate March–July Hot dry climate March–November Cool temperate climate March–November

Seed or seedling? Seed: sow in a pot and cover with seed-raising mix. Thin seedlings out as they develop.

I like . . . full to partial sun and well-draining soil.

I don't like . . . hot weather: pick any white flowers as they develop to prevent bolting; aphids.

Feed me . . . liquid fertiliser fortnightly.

Give me a drink . . . extremely fast-growing so needs frequent watering.

Pick me . . . pick while leaves are young, as if left the flavour can be overpowering.

Beef carpaccio with rocket

When a dish uses so few ingredients it requires each one to be the 'best in show'. Try to get your hands on some grass-fed, organic beef fillet for this classy starter (pictured opposite). You want the carpaccio to melt in your mouth.

Serves 6 as an entree

1 × 500 g lean beef fillet, trimmed of fat

⅓ cup (80 ml) extra virgin olive oil

juice of 1 lemon

salt and freshly ground black pepper

10–12 shavings parmesan

1 bunch rocket leaves, well washed and drained

- To make the beef easier to slice, chill it for half an hour or so in the freezer beforehand to firm it up, but do not let it freeze. Using a very sharp knife, carefully cut the beef into twelve very thin slices. Place each slice between two sheets of plastic film and gently beat with a meat mallet or other heavy object, taking care not to tear the meat.

- Arrange the beef slices on a large platter. Drizzle with oil and lemon juice and season with salt and pepper. Scatter over the parmesan shavings and top with a mound of rocket leaves. Finish with a final drizzle of oil and serve.

STRAWBERRY FIELDS FOREVER

If you only feel inclined to grow one edible on your balcony, it has got to be strawberries. They grow well in pots or hanging baskets and you get a good-sized crop from a small space. Growing your own strawberries organically will also cut down on the chemicals that enter your body. Strawberries – together with lettuces – are laced with pesticides and herbicides. Although tests by the consumer body Choice have found the levels in strawberries to be under acceptable current guidelines, the jury is still out on the cumulative effect all these chemicals are having on our bodies. We know it can't be good for us.

Strawberries should be sweet, juicy nuggets of goodness. They like a sunny position in rich, well-draining soil. Mine are sitting in a top-grade potting mix with wagyu poo and blood-and-bone mixed through. I've tucked some organic sugarcane straw mulch around them to prevent the emerging berries from rotting – which is what gives them their name strawberries.

I have two varieties growing: a large Tioga and the highly prized French variety Fraises du Bois. The latter is the variety you must search out (they can occasionally be found at suburban nurseries): the berries are small and sweet and have a heady rosewater perfume. Sadly the slugs know a good thing when they see it, too, and it's a constant battle finding and squishing them before they've burrowed into a luscious berry. I'm so thrilled to see the strawberries emerge from their white blossoms. They've perked me up no end. Winter hasn't been as bad as I feared. Glad it's almost over though.

I can feel the season turning. There's a friskiness in the air. New shoots and buds are peeping through. The days are getting longer and warmer. Newsflash, folks – spring is about to bloom.

Strawberries

When to plant? Hot humid climate Year-round **Hot dry climate** Year-round
Cool temperate climate Year-round

Seed or seedling? Buy certified disease-free plants from nurseries.

I like . . . lots of full sun; Dynamic Lifter added to well-draining soil.

I don't like . . . frost-sensitive when young; birds, snails and slugs.

Feed me . . . liquid fertiliser fortnightly while plants are fruiting.

Give me a drink . . . very thirsty, especially in hot weather.

Pick me . . . as fruit ripens. Each plant should last for three seasons.

Strawberry, Cointreau and vanilla-bean jam

When strawberries are plentiful, it calls for jam-making. Don't just use your strawberry jam to spread on toast in the mornings: put a dollop in your porridge, spoon some into mini baked pastry cases for an instant afternoon tea, or use it – thinned down with a little water – as a glaze for roasted quail. The possibilities are only limited by your imagination.

Makes 500 g

1 kg strawberries, hulled

1 kg sugar

3 vanilla beans, halved and seeds scraped

3 tablespoons Cointreau or your favourite orange liqueur

preserving jars, sterilised (see page 65)

- Place the strawberries in a large stockpot and add the sugar, vanilla beans and seeds and the liqueur and bring to the boil over medium heat. As the mixture begins to boil, slowly increase the heat to high and cook, stirring constantly, for 20–25 minutes. This jam doesn't 'set' like other jams due to the low pectin content in strawberries, so its final consistency will be a little runny.

- While still hot, spoon the jam into the prepared jars and leave to cool, then seal and store in a cool, dry place.

Grilled spatchcocks with strawberry salad

Serves 2

2 spatchcocks, butterflied

6–10 strawberries, halved

2 tablespoons Persian fetta

1 tablespoon pistachios, chopped

10 mint leaves

2 tablespoons pomegranate seeds

1 tablespoon olive oil

2 tablespoons dried rose petals

salt and freshly ground
black pepper

Marinade

2 cloves organic garlic

salt

3 tablespoons
pomegranate molasses

1 teaspoon ground cinnamon

½ onion, grated

pinch of ground allspice

Dressing

1 clove organic garlic, crushed

¼ teaspoon ground cinnamon

2 tablespoons
pomegranate molasses

⅓ cup (80 ml) extra virgin
olive oil

½ teaspoon caster sugar

salt and freshly ground
black pepper

A spatchcock is a small chicken or game bird. Spatchcock also describes the technique of splitting a bird along its backbone and flattening it for grilling or roasting (also known as 'butterflying').

You'll find the more unusual Middle Eastern ingredients used in this recipe at a good deli or spice store.

Due to the long marinating time, you'll need to start preparing this dish a day ahead.

- To make the marinade, first crush the garlic and a pinch of salt to a paste using a mortar and pestle. Add the rest of the marinade ingredients and rub all over the spatchcocks. Cover and refrigerate overnight.

- The next day, remove the spatchcocks from the fridge about half an hour before cooking to bring them to room temperature.

- In a large bowl, gently toss together the strawberries, fetta, pistachios, mint and pomegranate seeds.

- To make the dressing, mix the garlic with the cinnamon and pomegranate molasses, then add 1 tablespoon water and whisk in the olive oil. The dressing will thicken and emulsify. Add the sugar and season with salt and pepper to taste.

- Heat a barbecue grill plate to very hot. Brush the spatchcock with 1 tablespoon oil and grill for 5–8 minutes on each side or until cooked but still just pink and juicy in the centre. Season with salt and pepper as you turn them.

- Arrange the spatchcocks on a serving plate, and spoon around some strawberry salad. Sprinkle with rose petals and then drizzle with a little dressing.

Strawberry and white chocolate ganache tartlets

A fresh strawberry is sublime simplicity. Most of the ones I grew never made it to the kitchen – they went straight into my mouth. If you have more self-control than I do, these tartlets are a wonderful way to feature new season strawberries. I've used ready-made sweet pastry shells to cut down on the preparation time.

Makes 20

½ cup (125 ml) pouring cream

½ vanilla bean, seeds scraped

250 g good-quality Belgian white chocolate, roughly chopped

1 tablespoon unsalted butter, melted

20 ready-made sweet pastry tartlet cases

10 large strawberries, washed and dried well, cut into quarters

3 tablespoons good-quality strawberry jam, warmed

mint leaves, to garnish (optional)

- Place the cream and vanilla bean in the top of a double boiler or in a heatproof bowl placed over a saucepan of simmering water (making sure the bottom of the bowl does not touch the surface of the water). When the cream is simmering but not boiling, remove from the heat, take out the vanilla bean and add the chocolate. Stir to incorporate, then add the melted butter to give the ganache a shiny finish. Set aside to allow the ganache to cool and thicken.

- Lay out the pastry cases and spoon a dollop of cooled ganache into each one, then add two strawberry quarters. Brush with a little strawberry jam, top with a mint leaf if you like and serve for afternoon tea.

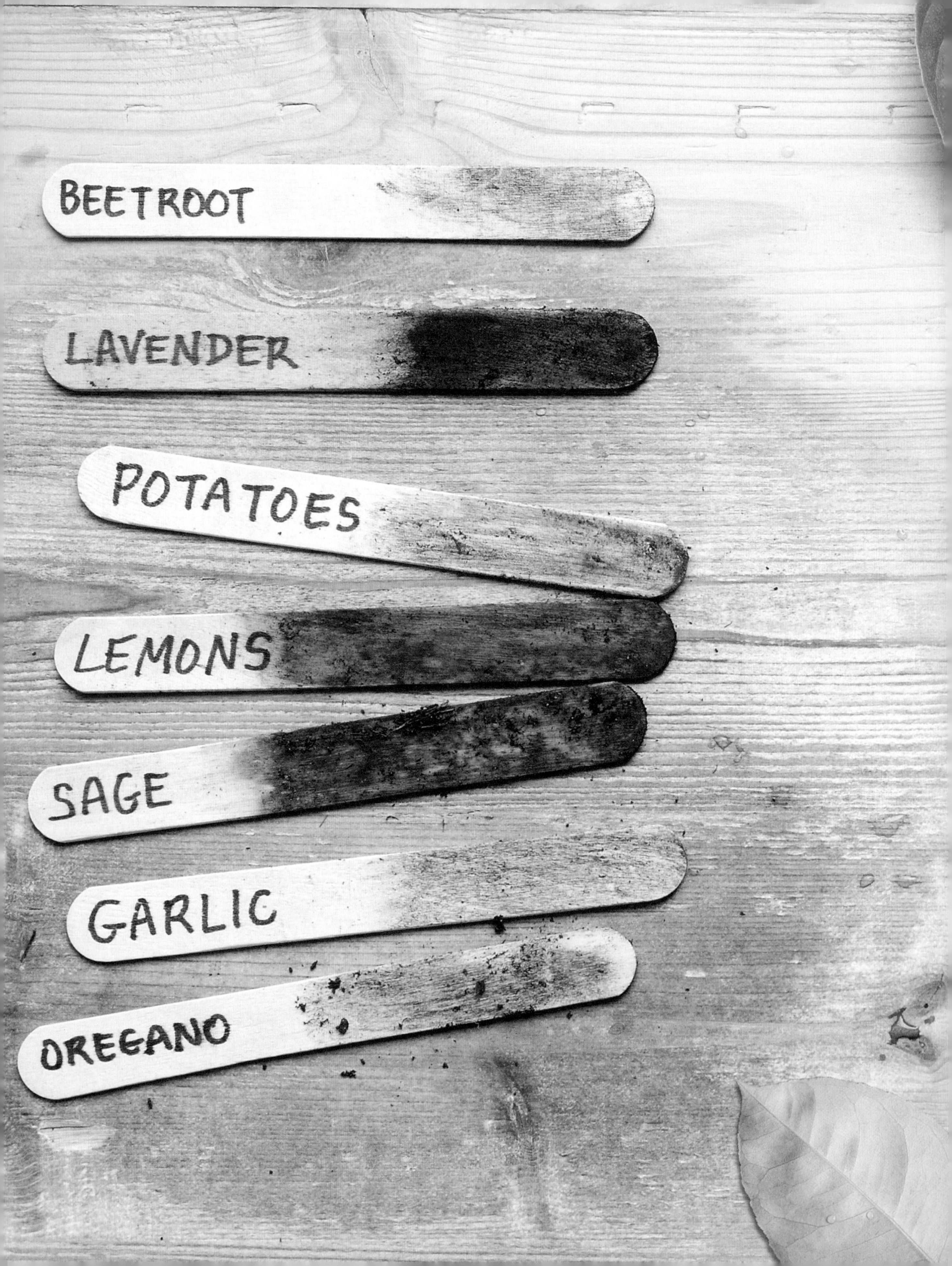
BEETROOT
LAVENDER
POTATOES
LEMONS
SAGE
GARLIC
OREGANO

SPRING

The plants are emerging from their winter hibernation with great gusto. The balcony is a riot of activity as insects and bees buzz about, pollinating new flower buds. It's the season for makin' whoopee.

A SPRING IN MY STEP

Is it safe to come out yet? That was one helluva winter: the coldest Sydney winter in several years, apparently. Not the best time to attempt an edible plant-growing experiment on a high-rise balcony. Mark says I've redefined madness. He may well be right. It was certainly the winter of my discontent – and possibly his. For three months, I followed online weather forecasts with a feverish obsession. I watched southerly busters roll over the harbour in a state of panic. A gust of wind or a grey cloud could flatten my spirits, if not the plants. Didn't anyone realise I was trying to *grow* things up here?

At least spring is here and hope, as they say, springs eternal. Most of the plants, even the ones that I feared were long dead, are reawakening. Crouched over the shrubbery, David Attenborough-style, I go in for a closer inspection. Yes, it's not a cruel hoax: there *are* new shoots emerging. Hallelujah! Stems I had thought of as gnarled bits of dead twig are sprouting green buds. The neon lights round the corner in Kings Cross should be flashing INDIRA'S PLANTS SURVIVE WINTER. Could this be Mary MacKillop's third miracle?

WHERE LEMON TREES BLOOM

The most romantic thing to grow on a terrace or balcony must be a lemon tree. Their intoxicatingly scented white flowers and sunshine-yellow fruit transport you straight to the Greek isles. It's no surprise to find that lemons are one of the most common edibles found in Australian backyards. Now that I've discovered how suitable they are for growing in pots, wouldn't it be breathtaking to see groves of potted lemons on balconies and rooftops, brightening up the drab city skyline?

While lemon trees are well suited to growing in a pot on a balcony, there are still some tricks to ensuring you'll get a bumper crop. First, select your lemon variety carefully. I planted a dwarf meyer lemon tree which, as the name suggests, is very compact. The fruit are a cross between a lemon and an orange. This makes them sweeter and less bitter than other lemon varieties. They also have a thin skin and lots of juice.

Make sure the pot you select is large enough to support the tree's root ball (about 30 cm in diameter should be ample); even dwarf lemon varieties need plenty of room to spread out. Place some gravel over the drainage holes at the base of the pot, and combine your potting mix with a little sand to ensure the soil drains well. Lemons don't like to compete with any grasses, so avoid mulching near the tree's trunk and immediate surface roots.

Lemons thrive in protected locations with at least six hours of sun a day. They don't like winds, so if your balcony is prone to the occasional draught, place your pot on a stand with wheels so you can easily move the tree as wind conditions change. They also hate having wet feet; another good reason to keep the pot off the ground. Water your lemon tree once or twice a week only, when the soil just below the surface feels dry. Feed it every 6 to 8 weeks with a citrus fertiliser and a good soaking.

Lemon trees, like most citrus, can fall prey to a range of pests and diseases and this can be a challenge for the organic gardener – it certainly was for me. Aphids (yes, those little buggers again) and other sap-sucking insects will cluster around new shoots. Zap them with pest oil. Sometimes citrus mites form a powdery coating that will attack your flower buds. Just pick off the damaged flowers and dispose of them so disease does not spread to the rest of the plant. Leaf miners are another headache. They leave little silvery trails on the leaves' undersides. They invaded my lemon tree in early winter and I needed several applications of pest oil to halt their assault. It left the leaves with patches of yellow, but it did kill *them varmints*. Leaves may also discolour from deficiencies of magnesium, iron or zinc, which can be treated with soluble powder treatments from your garden centre.

When your lemons are ready to harvest, here's a good tip to keep in mind. Lemons get juicier when they are stored for a few weeks, as the pith breaks down and releases more juice. If you want to store your lemons after harvesting, make sure a little of the stalk remains on each fruit when you pick them. This prevents bacteria entering through their 'cap'.

All this maintenance may sound like very demanding princess behaviour, but indulge your lemon tree as you would a teenage daughter, and the rewards will be a year-round bounty. Lemons are just such a versatile ingredient in so many cuisines. Their rind, pulp and juice can be used in an array of dishes, and even their leaves can be used, to flavour stews, to wrap ingredients in for cooking or to add to preserves and pickles.

Lemons

When to plant? Hot humid climate Any time except high summer Hot dry climate Any time, but autumn is best Cool temperate climate Autumn is best

Seed or seedling? Grafted trees.

I like . . . full sun, well-drained soil.

I don't like . . . competition around roots, and harsh cold.

Feed me . . . Dynamic Lifter in late February, and citrus food in early spring.

Give me a drink . . . regularly and deeply during summer when flowers are forming.

Pick me . . . fruit will last for a long time on tree. Store in a well-ventilated basket.

Preserved lemons

Preserved lemons should be a pantry staple. They are such a versatile way to add a lemony flavour to dishes as diverse as couscous, tagines, marinades or Sunday roast chicken. The flesh of the preserved lemon is generally discarded as it is too salty: the rind is then rinsed and finely chopped before being added to a dish.

Makes 3½ cups

5 unwaxed organic lemons, washed and dried thoroughly,
plus the juice from another 5–6 lemons, to cover

2 cups (300 g) coarse sea salt

1 large preserving jar, sterilised (see page 65)

5 cloves organic garlic

2 bay leaves

1 tablespoon coriander seeds

1 tablespoon cumin seeds

1 tablespoon black peppercorns

3 small dried red chillies

- Using a sharp knife, cut the five unwaxed lemons into quarters, almost to the base but not right through. Spread out the segments and pack each lemon with salt, then place it in the jar and squeeze down to release the juice. Pack a little more salt around each lemon as you put them in the jar.

- When the jar is filled with lemons, tip in the remaining salt, add the garlic, bay leaves and spices and top up with lemon juice to cover all the ingredients. Seal the jar and keep for at least 2 months in a cool, dry place before using. Once opened, the preserved lemons will keep in the fridge for up to 6 months.

Mini lemon curd cupcakes

Makes about 18

50 g butter, softened

¼ cup (55 g) caster sugar

½ teaspoon vanilla extract

1 organic egg

1 tablespoon milk

1 tablespoon lemon juice

½ cup (75 g)
self-raising flour

1 teaspoon finely grated
lemon zest

icing sugar, to dust

Lemon curd filling

4 organic egg yolks

½ cup (110 g) caster sugar

1 tablespoon finely grated
lemon zest

½ cup (125 ml) lemon juice

180 g cold unsalted
butter, chopped

These bite-sized cupcakes feature lemons both in the cupcake and in the lemon curd filling: you'll need 2–3 large lemons for this recipe. Lemon curd will keep in the fridge for up to two months. Also try it spread on toast or scones, as a tart filling with fresh raspberries or just straight from the jar!

- Preheat fan-forced oven to 180°C, and line two 12-hole mini muffin trays with patty pans.

- In an electric mixer, beat the butter, sugar, vanilla extract, egg, milk, lemon juice, flour and lemon zest on low speed until combined, then increase the speed to high and beat for 2 minutes until the mixture is pale and fluffy.

- Spoon teaspoonfuls of mixture into the patty pans and bake for 10 minutes or until a skewer inserted in the centre comes out clean. Remove from the oven, turn out and cool on wire racks.

- To make the lemon curd filling, place the egg yolks, sugar and lemon zest in the top of a double boiler or in a heatproof bowl placed over a saucepan of simmering water (making sure the bottom of the bowl does not touch the surface of the water). Whisk together until the sugar dissolves and the mixture turns pale. Add the lemon juice and whisk in, then add the butter, piece by piece, stirring until each piece has melted. Continue until all the butter has been combined and the mixture is thick. Remove from the heat and leave to cool before using.

- To assemble, take a cooled cupcake and, using a small sharp knife, cut out a small cone shape from the centre of the cake. Be careful not to cut through to the bottom. Fill the hole with a little lemon curd and place the cone back on top. Repeat with all the cupcakes and finish them with a dusting of icing sugar.

SAGE ADVICE

I'm curled up on the bench on the balcony, sipping a cup of sage tea, the morning sun gently warming my face. Sage doesn't make a bad cuppa – highly aromatic with a slightly bitter, astringent aftertaste. Make your own sage tea by placing a few of your homegrown leaves in the bottom of a cup and topping it up with hot water – not boiling water or you will destroy the beneficial antioxidants. Stir in a teaspoon of maple syrup if you need to sweeten your tea a little. Sage is a magical perennial herb believed to bring wisdom and strength to those who consume it. Chefs love to use it for the wonderful flavours it imparts to fish, veal and chicken, or when fried in sizzling nut-brown butter and served with pillows of fresh gnocchi.

Sage is tremendously hardy and almost impossible to kill off. Being a Mediterranean species, it doesn't require much water and thrives in well-draining soil in the full sun. There are many varieties; my tuft of sage is a long-leafed Russian variety with furry, silvery leaves that look like cats' tongues. It is growing in a hanging basket suspended from my balcony railing, flanked by yellow marigolds (it will produce its own seductive mauve flowers later in the season). It will grow happily in this position for three or four more years and then I'll need to take a cutting from the old bush and replant it.

Sage

When to plant? Hot humid climate March–August Hot dry climate August–March Cool temperate climate September–February

Seed or seedling? Seedling.

I like . . . full sun and well-draining soil.

I don't like . . . overcrowding.

Feed me . . . only occasionally, with a slow-release fertiliser.

Give me a drink . . . will tolerate dry conditions well.

Pick me . . . as required.

Sage, rosemary, celery and carrot juice

Looking for something a little different from your traditional morning OJ? This juice is packed with goodness, and the herbs provide a robust earthiness. For a variation, try green apples instead of the carrots, and throw in a piece of fresh ginger for extra zing.

Makes 2

small handful sage leaves

small handful rosemary leaves

8 sticks celery

3 carrots

ice cubes, to serve

- Put the sage, rosemary, celery and carrots through a juice extractor, adding the herbs first so the weight of the vegetables helps squeeze out all the juice from the herbs.

- Stir to combine and serve in a tall glass with some ice cubes.

Veal saltimbocca with sage butter

Serves a crowd

12 veal escalopes
(about 20 g each)

freshly ground black pepper

22 fresh sage leaves

12 slices prosciutto

12 toothpicks

plain flour, for dredging

100 g butter

⅓ cup (80 ml) olive oil

2 cloves organic
garlic, sliced

3 tablespoons dry
white wine

This is a consistent crowd-pleaser in my household. I use small escalopes to make bite-sized canapes, but you can use larger ones and serve this as an entree or a main course.

- Season the meat generously with pepper (there's no need to add salt as the prosciutto will be salty enough). Place a sage leaf on top of each piece of veal, reserving the rest for later, then wrap with a prosciutto slice and secure with a toothpick. Dredge the veal pieces in flour and shake off any excess.

- In a large heavy-based frying pan, melt half the butter with the oil over medium–high heat. Add 4 or 5 sage leaves and, working in batches, cook the veal for 2–3 minutes on each side, adding more olive oil as necessary. Transfer the cooked veal to a large plate and keep warm.

- Once all the veal is cooked, add the garlic and remaining sage leaves to the pan and fry for 1–2 minutes until the sage crisps up: you may need to add a little more butter. Remove the crispy sage leaves and set aside.

- Pour in the wine, increase the heat to high and cook for 5 minutes or until reduced by half, scraping all the tasty bits from the bottom of the pan.

- To serve, arrange the veal slices on a large platter, spoon over the butter sauce and scatter over the crispy sage leaves.

Sage and cheddar biscuits

These savoury biscuits are soft and crumbly. I serve them as part of a cheeseboard with olives and salami, or just on their own with a glass of white wine. They're also great for kids' lunchboxes.

Makes 24

150 g butter, softened

1½ cups (225 g) plain flour, plus extra for dusting

125 g sharp cheddar cheese, grated

small handful finely chopped sage leaves, plus extra to garnish (optional)

pinch of salt

½ teaspoon cayenne pepper

½ teaspoon mustard powder

- Place all the ingredients except the whole sage leaves in a large mixing bowl and beat with a wooden spoon until the mixture comes together. Transfer mixture to a clean, floured benchtop, divide in half and roll into two logs about 3 cm thick. Wrap in plastic film and refrigerate for 30 minutes.

- Meanwhile, preheat fan-forced oven to 180°C and line two large baking sheets with baking paper.

- Slice the logs into discs about 1–2 cm thick and place on the prepared baking sheets. Press a sage leaf onto a few biscuits, if desired. Bake for 10–12 minutes until just slightly browned.

MasterChef meatballs

Serves 6

250 g organic minced veal

250 g organic minced pork

250 g organic minced lamb

4 cloves organic garlic, crushed

2 tablespoons fresh breadcrumbs

1 organic egg, beaten

½ cup (100 g) fresh ricotta

¼ cup (20 g) grated parmesan

¼ cup flat-leaf parsley, finely chopped

¼ cup basil, finely chopped

salt and freshly ground black pepper

2 tablespoons extra virgin olive oil

1 onion, finely chopped

1 bay leaf

1 anchovy fillet

1 x 750 ml bottle tomato passata

1 x 400 g can chopped tomatoes

1 teaspoon sugar

My meatballs have always been a crowd pleaser, so they were the obvious choice to cook as my 'signature dish' when I appeared in the inaugural series of Network Ten's *Celebrity MasterChef* in 2009.

Unfortunately, under the pressure of all the cameras and lights and a ticking clock – not to mention a million viewers – I went to jelly and, in my panic, I overcooked my meatballs. While George and Gary liked them, Matt said they were 'a little spongy', and I was bundled out of the competition.

Humiliating as the experience was, it did make me a better cook. And, rest assured, I have made these meatballs several times since and they are always moist and delicious. Ricotta cheese is the magic ingredient.

- Combine the minced meat, garlic, breadcrumbs, beaten egg, ricotta, parmesan and herbs in a large bowl and season well with salt and pepper. Using clean hands, mix until well combined, then shape into twenty meatballs. Place the meatballs on a plate, cover with plastic film and refrigerate for 10 minutes.

- Meanwhile, heat the oil in a large heavy-based saucepan over medium heat. Add the onion, bay leaf and anchovy and cook for 5 minutes or until the onion has softened. Stir in the passata, chopped tomatoes and sugar, reduce the heat to low and simmer for 20 minutes. Season to taste.

- Add the meatballs to the hot sauce and simmer over very low heat for 10–15 minutes, until the meatballs are just cooked, but still very soft and moist.

continued over page →

Polenta

2 cups (500 ml)
chicken stock

1 cup (170 g)
instant polenta

½ cup (40 g)
grated parmesan

2 tablespoons butter

Pesto oil

1 bunch basil, leaves picked

1 clove organic
garlic, chopped

½ cup (80 g) pine
nuts, toasted

½ teaspoon salt

1 cup (250 ml)
extra virgin olive oil

¼ cup (20 g)
grated parmesan

¼ cup (20 g)
grated pecorino

- To make the polenta, bring the stock and 2 cups (500 ml) water to the boil in a large saucepan over medium–high heat. Pour in the polenta in a slow, steady stream, stirring continuously until the mixture thickens and boils. Continue cooking the polenta, stirring, for a further 10 minutes. Add the cheese and butter and stir well. The mixture should be wet and have the consistency of porridge. Set aside in a warm place.

- For the pesto oil, place the basil leaves, garlic, pine nuts and ½ teaspoon salt in a food processor and blend until smooth. With the motor running, pour in the oil in a steady stream until combined. Stir in the grated cheeses and adjust the seasoning to taste.

- To serve, place some polenta on a plate, top with two or three meatballs and some tomato sauce. Drizzle with pesto oil to finish.

GARLIC UPDATE: IT WILL TAKE YOUR BREATH AWAY

I planted my garlic bulbs back in May. And then I did a lot of waiting. And waiting. And waiting.

Over winter, not a lot seemed to happen. The bulbs threw up long reed-like leaves that formed two fans. The bottom ones turned yellow and withered and were replaced by new leaves. The stalks of two of the plants became thicker and woodier, while the others remained slender. In spring, the earth around the stalk started to push up – a sign that the bulbs were starting to fill out and develop.

Work called me overseas again, so I thought I'd delay harvesting my garlic until my return. This decision could have been the biggest mistake of my year-long edible gardening experiment. Back on the balcony in early December, with delirious anticipation, I excitedly loosened the soil around my garlic leaves and gently pulled out the first garlic plant. But instead of seeing a bunch of papery, purple garlic bulbs attached to the stems, all I found were long white roots, similar to those of a leek. Horrified, I quickly pulled out the other plants and found the same thing – no garlic! Six long months of watering, feeding and waiting had resulted in a failed crop.

The disappointment was gut-wrenching. Where had I stuffed up? I sought advice from my garlic supplier and realised I had possibly left my plants in too long, and the bulbs had converted back into roots. My garlic's leaves had started yellowing in early November and that's when I should have harvested them.

My mate, the award-winning chef and food educator Stefano Manfredi, came to the rescue. He had just harvested a wonderfully pungent crop of garlic from his kitchen garden and very generously gave me some to use in my summer dishes. They were so delicious in my meatballs that, after a little emotional healing, I will be attempting to grow garlic again next year. After all, it couldn't happen to me two years running, could it?

I ♥ LAVENDER

Painters and poets through the ages have been driven to distraction by lavender. Monet, Van Gogh, Lord Byron and Jackson Pollock all fell under its spell. They were captivated by what gardeners have always known; if love were a plant, it would be lavender. It's one of the most versatile of all edible garden plants. Pretty to look at, an intoxicating scent, a bee attractant, and used to flavour, colour and decorate food. What's not to love?

Lavender is part of the rosemary family and therefore requires similar growing conditions. It needs plenty of sun, well-draining soil and is fairly drought-tolerant.

Pick the flowers as they die off to encourage new growth, and give your plant a thorough prune in winter so your lavender bush will burst forth with new flower buds for spring.

Lavender

When to plant? Hot humid climate Year-round **Hot dry climate** Year-round Cool temperate climate Year-round

Seed or seedling? Seed, seedling or from a cutting. Best to plant in spring or summer when weather is warmer.

I like . . . full sun and dry, well-draining soil.

I don't like . . . too much water, wind or frost.

Feed me . . . only occasionally.

Give me a drink . . . once or twice a week.

Pick me . . . as flowers appear. Regular pruning will encourage new growth.

Chocolate fondants with lavender cream

Makes 6

350 g dark chocolate, roughly chopped

50 g butter, softened

¾ cup (150 g) caster sugar

4 organic eggs

2 tablespoons plain flour

Lavender cream

1 tablespoon caster sugar

1 cup (250 ml) thickened cream

5–6 lavender flower buds, flowers removed

These fondants can be made a day ahead and kept in the fridge. Bring them to room temperature and pop them into the oven 20 minutes before you want to serve them.

- To make the lavender cream, whisk the sugar and cream together for a couple of minutes until the sugar has dissolved. Stir in the lavender flower buds and chill in the fridge for an hour to allow the flavours to infuse.

- Preheat fan-forced oven to 180°C, grease six 125 ml ramekins and place them on a baking tray.

- Melt the chocolate in the top of a double boiler or in a heatproof bowl placed over a saucepan of simmering water (making sure the bottom of the bowl does not touch the surface of the water).

- In a large mixing bowl, beat the butter and sugar until light and fluffy, then add the eggs one by one, beating after each addition. Add the flour and mix well. Add the melted chocolate and combine to form a smooth batter.

- Divide the mixture evenly between the six ramekins. (If you're not going to cook them straight away, cover and chill them at this point.) Place the tray in the oven and cook for 18–20 minutes. Check them by inserting a skewer in the centre: they should still be gooey and runny in the middle, but cooked around the edges to a width of at least 1 cm.

- When cooked, remove from the oven, loosen around the sides with a knife and turn the fondants out onto plates. Serve with a large dollop of lavender cream.

Lavender panna cotta with wild honey

Gelatine is a setting agent that comes in powdered or leaf form. I prefer the titanium-strength leaf which gives a smoother consistency. You can buy gelatine leaves from good delicatessens and cooking supply stores.

Makes 6

600 ml pouring cream

400 ml double cream

½ cup (125 ml) wild honey

10 fresh lavender flowers, plus extra to garnish

3 leaves titanium-strength gelatine

- Place the creams in a large saucepan, stirring to combine. Add the honey and lavender flowers and bring to a simmer over low heat for 5 minutes to allow the flavours to infuse.

- Meanwhile, soak the gelatine leaves in a bowl of cold water for about 5 minutes and, once softened, squeeze out the excess water and add the leaves to the cream mixture. Remove from the heat and stir through. Allow to cool slightly then strain the mixture through a fine sieve. Pour into dariole moulds, cover and refrigerate for 3–4 hours until set.

- To loosen, run a knife round the inside of the mould then dip the mould into hot water for 5 seconds. Place a plate on top and invert, and serve garnished with a lavender flower.

OREGANO – THE TASTE OF THE MEDITERRANEAN

All the countries and cultures that hug the expansive coastline of the Mediterranean use oregano leaves, both fresh and dried, in their cuisines. A Greek salad just wouldn't be the same without them; an Italian tomato sauce would have no zing; and Turkish grilled lamb would lack its characteristic earthiness.

This humble herb, which originated high in the mountains of Greece, is a hardy perennial that can take quite a bit of abuse and neglect from a novice balcony gardener. Give your oregano plant plenty of sun in well-draining soil and a liquid fertiliser during the spring/ summer growing season. As with lavender, cut your oregano plant back in winter to encourage new spring growth. And before you know it, some of the greatest cuisines of the world will be at your fingertips.

Oregano

When to plant? Hot humid climate Year-round Hot dry climate July–August Cool temperate climate August–March

Seed or seedling? Seed.

I like . . . well-draining soil in full sun.

I don't like . . . shade.

Feed me . . . liquid fertiliser during main growing season in late spring and summer.

Give me a drink . . . quite drought-hardy but requires regular watering in summer.

Pick me . . . as required.

Marinated olives with oregano, garlic and preserved lemon

Fresh oregano is very pungent, which is why many cooks prefer using it in its dried form. But when you're marinating olives and require big flavours, only fresh oregano will do. Its long curving sprigs also look very attractive in your olive jar.

Makes 500 g

½ cup (125 ml) extra virgin olive oil

3 tablespoons white-wine vinegar

1 tablespoon lemon juice

4 preserved lemon quarters, rind thinly sliced

2 cloves organic garlic, sliced

5 sprigs fresh oregano

2 cups (450 g) green Sicilian olives, drained

1 large preserving jar, sterilised (see page 65)

- In a small saucepan, heat the oil, vinegar, lemon juice, preserved lemon, garlic and oregano over low heat for 5 minutes.

- Place the olives in a bowl and pour the flavourings over. Leave to stand for 2–3 hours at room temperature for the flavours to infuse before using.

- The olives can be eaten straight away or stored in the prepared jar in the fridge for 2–3 weeks. Their flavours will deepen over time.

MR POTATO HEAD

I'm having a lot of fun growing my potatoes. I know many people think you can just throw the old potatoes from your pantry into some soil *et, voilà!* more potatoes. But it's not quite that simple.

It's important to find certified organic seed potatoes from a reputable grower. This ensures that your potatoes have been inspected for diseases. (Seed potatoes cannot be sent through the mail to some states due to quarantine restrictions – check what the rules are where you live.) Once your seeds begin to sprout from the eyes of the potato, you're ready to plant. The best time is two or three weeks after the last frost in your area. I'm growing my crop in planter bags made from recycled plastic. These bags are worth investing in because they're light and durable, with ready-made drainage holes. They're also easy to store between growing seasons.

Potatoes love good drainage and well-fertilised soils, layered with mulch and potting mix. So into my bags first went some sugarcane mulch, then some aged manure (Gundooee Organics poo again) then my spuds, about four in each bag, and finally some blood-and-bone and some potting mix. After 2–3 weeks, when the first green shoots are just visible, repeat this layering process, and when the next potato shoots poke through, cover them again with more layers. By covering the shoots this way and preventing light from penetrating, you will encourage more potatoes to root. Depending on the size of your planter you should get three to four layers of potatoes in each container.

Potatoes will take about three months to mature. You'll know when they are ready when the plant's lower leaves begin to yellow. Harvest them straight away (as new potatoes) or leave them a little longer for larger ones with thicker skins.

The varieties you grow will depend on the ones you like to eat. I've planted the banana variety which is small, tinged with yellow and slightly curved, hence the name. I've also popped in some good ol' reliable desirees, symphonias and the gorgeously vibrant royal blue. Within ten days, I spied green potato shoots peeping through the soil, and within about four weeks big-leafed stalks had sprawled to cover 1 square metre. Only one of my plants flowered but it didn't affect my yield so don't panic if yours don't.

My planter bags produced about 5 kilos of potatoes. Throughout spring and early summer, we had them boiled, mashed or roasted, culminating in our annual Christmas Day extravagance of super crunchy potatoes baked in duck fat – our once-a-year, artery-clogging treat.

Potatoes

When to plant? Hot humid climate January–August **Hot dry climate** July–October, January–February **Cool temperate climate** August–December

Seed or seedling? Select specially bred, disease-free 'seed' potatoes from a nursery or produce supplier. Don't use the old mouldy ones from your pantry!

I like . . . well-draining soil with plenty of manure and blood-and-bone at time of planting; lots of sun.

I don't like . . . frosts; potato moths and aphids.

Feed me . . . can fertilise again but only a little is needed.

Give me a drink . . . regularly.

Pick me . . . small new potatoes can be harvested when the bottom leaves turn yellow. Leave longer for larger older potatoes.

Potato skordalia

Potato skordalia is a wonderful accompaniment to grilled meats, poached fish or grilled vegetables. A waxy variety of potato, such as dutch cream or desiree, works best in this recipe.

Makes 1 cup

2 large potatoes, cut into chunks

3 cloves organic garlic, roughly chopped

1 teaspoon salt

2 organic egg yolks

½–¾ cup (125–180 ml) extra virgin olive oil

2 tablespoons freshly squeezed lemon juice

freshly ground black pepper

- Bring a large saucepan of salted water to the boil and add the potato. Simmer, uncovered, until the potato is soft when pierced with a skewer. Drain and place back in the pan over low heat for a few seconds to dry out further. Mash well then transfer to a bowl, cover and set aside.

- Pound the garlic with the salt using a mortar and pestle until you have a smooth paste. Add this to the potato puree and stir through. Beat in the egg yolks, one at a time, then gradually pour in the oil, mixing after each addition: you should end up with a thick, dense paste. Stir through the lemon juice and season to taste with pepper before serving.

Super crunchy roasted potatoes

As this recipe calls for duck fat, it definitely does not get the Heart Foundation's tick of approval. So that we can feel good about our indulgence, we usually only have these extraordinary-tasting potatoes once a year with our Christmas dinner. It's why we all look forward to Christmas so much! You can buy duck fat in cans or jars from good butchers and delis.

Serves 8 as part of a main course

2 kg desiree potatoes, chopped in half

½ cup duck fat

2 tablespoons salt

handful rosemary sprigs

- Preheat fan-forced oven to 180°C.

- Bring a large saucepan of salted water to the boil and add the halved potatoes. Simmer, uncovered, until the potatoes are just soft when pierced with a skewer but not cooked through. Drain well, then return the potatoes to the pan, place the lid on and shake the pan to break up the potatoes slightly; this helps them to absorb the duck fat while they are roasting.

- Spoon the duck fat into a large roasting pan and place in the oven for 2 minutes until hot but not smoking. Remove the pan from the oven and carefully toss in the potatoes, making sure they are well coated with fat, then scatter over the salt and rosemary sprigs.

- Bake for around 1 hour, tossing the pan occasionally, until they are crunchy and golden.

BEETROOT – CAN THE CAN

Sadly, for most children of my generation the first encounter with beetroot we had was not a pleasant one. Beetroot came only one way: in a can. It tasted of harsh vinegar and not much else. It bled all over your boiled-egg sandwich in your lunchbox. Everything within its vicinity turned mushy and pink.

Fresh beetroot couldn't be more different. Young baby beets grated raw in a salad and tossed with roasted hazelnuts, goat's cheese and salad greens have a far superior texture and taste than those tinned spongy slices soaked in acid. When these crimson globes are fresh they are crunchy and earthy and beautifully ring-barked with the faintest of stripes.

The most commonly grown beetroot is deep red and round, but beetroot also comes in white, yellow and candy-striped varieties. Beetroot can grow throughout the year in a temperate climate, but I planted my seeds in late winter so I could enjoy a spring crop. As your seeds sprout, thin them out, remembering not to crowd the plants so your beets can have plenty of room to bulk up.

They're fast growers, needing only a well-manured potting mix and regular watering. Hold back on the nitrogen fertilisers or you'll get lots of leafy growth but small beets. Beetroot leaves make a tasty salad green; just make sure to pick the leaves while they are small and young or they may be a little bitter.

Beetroot

When to plant? Hot humid climate Year-round **Hot dry climate** January–April, August–December **Cool temperate climate** January–April, September–December

Seed or seedling? Grows better from seed. Soak seeds overnight before planting.

I like . . . well-draining, well-manured soil.

I don't like . . . the cold.

Feed me . . . once a fortnight with a low-nitrogen fertiliser.

Give me a drink . . . regularly, particularly in hot weather.

Pick me . . . in 8–10 weeks.

Aussie beef burgers with beetroot

Serves 4

500 g minced beef

1 onion, finely chopped

2 cloves organic garlic, crushed

1 organic egg, lightly beaten

1 tablespoon dried breadcrumbs

small handful each of flat-leaf parsley and basil leaves, finely chopped

salt and freshly ground black pepper

olive oil, for brushing

1 tablespoon wasabi mayonnaise

4 hamburger buns, halved

4 iceberg lettuce leaves

1 ox-heart tomato, sliced

Baked beetroot

1 bunch baby beetroot, washed thoroughly and trimmed leaving 5 cm stalk

10 cloves organic garlic, unpeeled

⅓ cup (80 ml) olive oil

3 tablespoons balsamic vinegar

1 tablespoon chopped oregano

salt and freshly ground black pepper

If you're like me and think a burger isn't a real burger without beetroot, you'll be wowed when you try them with fresh beetroot instead of the canned variety.

I keep these patties ready-made in the freezer for a quick dinner – just thaw and reheat them. The uncooked patties can also be frozen, and all you need to do for a no-effort cocktail nibble is thaw them, roll them into little meatballs and shallow-fry them.

- To prepare the beetroot, preheat fan-forced oven to 200°C.

- Spread out a large square of kitchen foil and shape into a bowl to fit all the beetroot. Add the beetroot, garlic, olive oil, balsamic, oregano and salt and pepper to taste. Seal the foil over the ingredients. Bake for 1 hour or until the beetroot are soft when pierced with a skewer. Remove from the oven and when they are cool enough to handle, remove their skins with your fingers. Be careful – red beetroot can stain, so use plastic food-handling gloves if you like. Slice the beetroot and set aside while you prepare the burgers.

- In a large bowl, combine the minced beef, onion, garlic, egg, breadcrumbs, herbs and season with salt and pepper. Fashion the mixture into four palm-sized patties and leave to rest in the fridge for 30 minutes (you can wrap the patties in plastic film and freeze them at this stage for cooking another time).

- Heat a barbecue grill plate to very hot. Brush the burgers with oil and cook for 3 minutes on one side and 5 minutes on the other side. Turn over again and as soon as you see red juices bubbling to the surface, take the burgers off the heat if you like them medium–rare (if you like them well-done, cook for a little longer). Leave the burgers to rest for a minute or two after cooking.

- To assemble, spread a little wasabi mayonnaise over the buns, and stack with some lettuce, sliced tomato, a burger and some beetroot slices. Top with a bun lid and serve.

Beetroot and wasabi relish

Wasabi is a type of Japanese horseradish that is grown commercially in Victoria and Tasmania. Most of the harvest is exported to the Japanese market but occasionally you can find fresh wasabi root in some greengrocers and at farmers' markets. Fresh wasabi will give you a better result in this recipe, so try and seek it out, but remember it has a bigger bang than the paste, so you'll need less. And if you live in cool climes, why not try growing it on your balcony!

Enjoy this relish smeared onto some flatbread for a delicious appetiser or as an accompaniment to roast beef.

Makes 300 g

4 medium-sized beetroot or 8 baby beetroot, washed thoroughly and trimmed, leaving 5 cm stalk

¼ cup (60 g) creme fraiche

1 teaspoon grated fresh wasabi *or* 1 tablespoon wasabi paste

1 tablespoon lemon juice

1 teaspoon Dijon mustard

salt and freshly ground black pepper

- Cook the beetroot over high heat in a large pan of water for about 10–15 minutes or until soft. Drain and set aside until they are cool enough to handle, then remove their skins with your fingers. Be careful – red beetroot can stain, so use plastic food-handling gloves if you like.

- Chop the beetroot into small pieces and place in a food processor with all the other ingredients. Pulse until you have a thick, rough-textured sauce. Taste and adjust the seasoning. This relish will keep in an airtight container in the fridge for 2–3 weeks.

FROM LITTLE THINGS, BIG THINGS GROW

My beetroot crop marked the end of the spring season – and the end of my year-long edible balcony experiment. From an initial investment of just $200 on soil, pots, tools, seeds and fertiliser, I produced about 72 kilos of food from 43 types of herbs and vegetables. Not bad for a 20-square-metre concrete 'farm', thirteen floors off the ground.

When I began my edible balcony project a year ago, I thought it would mean sacrificing my social life for hours of watering, pruning and spraying. What I discovered was that after the initial time it took to establish the garden (just one weekend), I only needed to spend 10 minutes a day to get very good results. This daily spot-check is how you tackle trouble before it sets in and it's how you notice the small changes that may need your attention. That's the wonderful thing about gardening – it teaches you to be present and attentive. It makes you stop and focus on something that is outside of yourself. It's also incredibly relaxing. I'm discovering that the best antidote to a tough day at the office is not always a stiff gin and tonic; stepping out onto my balcony, smelling the herbs, touching new leaves and breathing in their oxygen is an equally soothing elixir.

Without exception, the herbs, fruit and vegetables I grow myself taste better than anything I could buy at a super-market – sometimes even better than produce from a farmers' market. I still marvel at the convenience of having a vegie patch right on my doorstep. There is no substitute for pesticide-free, just-picked-a-moment-ago produce when it comes to flavour and nutrition, and watching something grow

From barren beginnings...

only increases your appetite to eat it. My edibles also had an impact on what I cooked. Instead of turning to a cookbook for inspiration, before planning a meal I surveyed the balcony to see what was ripe and ready for harvesting. In this way my cooking became truly seasonal.

There will always be food essentials you cannot grow yourself: this is when the principles of your edible balcony can be applied. Eat what is freshest and local for the best flavour and nutrition, and this will also reduce the impact of carbon emissions resulting from transportation. This is often called locavore eating. If pantry staples such as olive oil, parmesan cheese or salt are not available locally, seek them out from other regions that apply these organic, seasonal principles.

I will continue growing herbs and vegetables on my balcony. I've found the experience unexpectedly rewarding and life-changing. We need to be reminded in our busy city lives that everything has a time and a purpose. My edibles have taught me a very important lesson: I am not separate from nature – I am *part* of nature. As much as I have enjoyed growing such a wide variety of edibles, next year I plan to grow just my favourites; plenty of fresh herbs (especially basil), rocket, lettuces and tubs and tubs of tomatoes. My edible balcony is here to stay. Sorry Mark. (Although, just between you and me, I don't think he minds all that much actually.)

Long before self-help books and television advertising, humans instinctively knew what to eat and how to eat it. How else could we have survived so well for the past 200 000 years? Sadly, my generation was the first of the latchkey kids who missed out on having this important food knowledge passed down to them. And my generation was the first to suffer the consequences; obesity, diabetes and heart disease and, just as importantly, a disconnection from where our food really came from.

...to a lush, productive garden.

Reclaiming what we have lost is no small challenge. How can you know what you do not know? Supermarkets have given us convenience but in many ways they have taken away our choice. What if you don't want to eat vegetables that have been sprayed with chemicals? What if you don't want to eat an apple that has been stored for 8 months? What if you want to reduce your carbon footprint by mostly eating what is grown in your local area, not on the other side of the world? What if taste is more important to you than cost?

To have a real effect on these issues, we can no longer see ourselves purely as consumers of food; we need to become *producers* of our food as well. Of course, as city dwellers we will never be able to grow everything we eat, but the simple act of growing a small pot of herbs is how this reconnection with our food can begin.

If you want to change the world, change what you put on your plate. And if you want to change *your* world, start an edible balcony today.

SUPPLIERS

Seeds

Four Seasons Herbs
PO Box 110, Exeter TAS 7275
0412 721 268
fourseasonsherbs.com.au

The Diggers Club
PO Box 300, Dromana VIC 3936
(03) 5984 7900
diggers.com.au

The Italian Gardener
PO Box 379, Figtree NSW 2525
0407 833 930
theitaliangardener.com.au

The Lost Seed
PO Box 321, Sheffield TAS 7306
(03) 6491 1000
thelostseed.com.au

Seedlings

Bunnings
Stores nationwide
bunnings.com.au

Eden Gardens
301–307 Lane Cove Road, North Ryde
NSW 2113
(02) 9491 9900
edengardens.com.au

Four Seasons Herbs
(See listing under 'Seeds' opposite)

Garden Life
357 Cleveland Street, Surry Hills
NSW 2016
(02) 9491 9900
gardenlife.com.au

Other

The Balcony Gardener
(gardening equipment)
thebalconygardener.com

Bugs For Bugs
(07) 4165 4663
bugsforbugs.com.au

Garden Boutique
(gardening equipment)
gardenboutique.co.uk

Grow-your-own mushroom kits
fungi.net.au

Heaven in Earth
(gardening equipment)
77 Hakea Close, Nowra NSW 2541
heaveninearth.com.au

BIBLIOGRAPHY

Albert, Stephen, *The Kitchen Garden Growers Guide: A Practical Vegetable and Herb Garden Encyclopedia*, BookSurge Publishing, South Carolina, 2008.

Alexander, Stephanie, *The Cook's Companion*, 2nd edn, Lantern, Melbourne, 2004.

An Inconvenient Truth. Dir. Davis Guggenheim, Writer Al Gore, Paramount Classics, 2006.

Barker, Barbara, *Container Gardening For Health*, Prairie Oak Publishing, Maryville, 2009.

Bartholomew, Mel, *All New Square Foot Gardening: Grow More in Less Space*, Cool Springs Press, Tennessee, 2006.

Bradley, Fern Marshall, Barbara Ellis & Deborah L. Martin (eds.), *The Organic Gardener's Handbook of Natural Insect and Disease Control*, Rodale Press, United States, 2010.

Carpenter, Novella, *Farm City: The Education of an Urban Farmer*, Penguin Press, New York, 2009.

Davis, Margaret, *Balcony, Terrace and Patio Gardening*, Fulcrum Publishing, Colorado, 1997.

Kingsolver, Barbara, Camille Kingsolver & Steven L.Hopp, *Animal, Vegetable, Miracle: A Year of Food Life*, Harper Collins, New York, 2007.

Lamb, Harriet, *Fighting The Banana Wars and Other Fairtrade Battles*, Random House, Great Britain, 2008.

Lynas, Mark, *Carbon Counter*, Harper Collins, Australia, 2007.

Patel, Raj, *Stuffed and Starved*, Black Inc. Books, Australia, 2009.

Petrini, Carlo, *Slow Food Nation: Why Our Food Should be Good, Clean and Fair*, Rizzoli Ex Libris, 2007.

Pollan, Michael, *Second Nature: A Gardener's Education*, Bloomsbury, London, 1996.

——, *The Omnivore's Dilemma: A Natural History of Four Meals*, Penguin Press, New York, 2000.

——, *In Defense of Food: An Eater's Manifesto*, Penguin Press, New York, 2008.

——, *Food Rules: An Eater's Manual*, Penguin UK, London, 2010.

Reader's Digest (eds.), *Foods That Harm: Foods That Heal*, (2004).

Richardson, Jill, *A Taste Of The Bush: Rainforest to Table*, 2009.

Schlosser, Eric, *Fast Food Nation: The Dark Side of the All-American Meal*, Houghton Mifflin, New York, 2001.

Shiva, Vandana, *Earth Democracy: Justice, Sustainability and Peace*, South End Press, Massachusetts, 2005

——, *Soil Not Oil: Environmental Justice in an Age of Climate Crisis*, South End Press, Massachusetts, 2008.

Smith, Alisa & J.B. Mackinnon, *Plenty: Eating Locally on the 100 Mile Diet*, Three Rivers Press, New York, 2007.

Smith, C. Edward, *The Vegetable Gardener's Bible (10th Anniversary edn)*, Storey Publishing, Massachusetts, 2010.

Zissu, Alexandra, *The Conscious Kitchen*, Clarkson Potter, New York, 2010.

Internet resources

ABC1's *Gardening Australia* website: *abc.net.au/gardening*

Bugs For Bugs: *bugsforbugs.com.au/about/bugs-for-bugs*

Carbon Trust UK: *carbontrust.co.uk*

The Food and Farming Transition: Toward a Post Carbon Food System by Michael Bomford & Richard Heinberg, report can be downloaded at *postcarbon.org/food*

Food Inc: *FoodIncMovie.com*

The Guardian UK: *guardian.co.uk/lifeandstyle/gardens*

Intergovernmental Panel on Climate Change: *ipcc.ch/*

Royal Horticultural Society, UK: *rhs.org.uk/Gardening*

WHO's twenty questions and answers on genetically modified foods: *WHO.int/foodsafety/publications/biotech/20questions/en*

ACKNOWLEDGEMENTS

I learnt many things during the writing of this, my first book.

I discovered why it is important to write what you are passionate about. How else do words appear on your blank computer screen at four o'clock in the morning!

I also discovered why it is important to surround yourself with a group of specialists you can go running to when it all gets too much (as it inevitably will).

My hand-holders throughout these past two years have been an extraordinary collective of photographers, designers, editors, publishers, gardeners, horticulturalists, farmers, chefs, agents, food writers, journalists – and of course my long-suffering family and friends.

To everyone at Penguin, thank you for your encouragement, guidance and profess-ionalism. Thank you to Ingrid Ohlsson, Kirby Armstrong, Emily O'Neill, Megan Pigott, Sophie Geoghegan, Katie Quinn Davies, Virginia Birch, my inspirational editor, and especially Julie Gibbs for giving me the opportunity to create a book of which I am so proud.

My photographer, Alan Benson, was there with me every step of the way. His luminous photography, enthusiasm, recipe taste-testing and friendship made this project a pure joy. This book is as much his creation as it is mine (except he doesn't get any royalties, as he keeps reminding me). You're the best, Benson.

A huge thank you to Jock Gammon of Junglefy who installed my vertical wall unit, and Rob and Nita Lennon of Gundooee Organics who supplied me with my organic cow poo.

Big kisses, also, to the gorgeous concierges in my building – Darrell, Kevin, Chris, Ahmed and John – who did such a terrific job of looking after my plants whenever I was away.

To Jennifer and Beverley at my agency, RGM Artist Group, thank you for all your wonderful advice and encouragement.

And to my dear husband Mark FitzGerald who, during the past two years, has had to share our apartment with an assortment of props, boards, lights, photographic equipment, and teams of designers and stylists, not to mention all the plants! Thank you for your unwavering support throughout the writing of this book. I could not have done it without you.

And, last but not least, to the real stars of this book – all the plants, herbs, fruit and vegetables on my balcony who, hopefully, will continue to grow, thrive and nourish my family.

INDEX

LANTERN

Published by the Penguin Group
Penguin Group (Australia)
250 Camberwell Road, Camberwell, Victoria 3124, Australia
(a division of Pearson Australia Group Pty Ltd)
Penguin Group (USA) Inc.
375 Hudson Street, New York, New York 10014, USA
Penguin Group (Canada)
90 Eglinton Avenue East, Suite 700, Toronto, Canada ON M4P 2Y3
(a division of Pearson Penguin Canada Inc.)
Penguin Books Ltd
80 Strand, London WC2R 0RL England
Penguin Ireland
25 St Stephen's Green, Dublin 2, Ireland
(a division of Penguin Books Ltd)
Penguin Books India Pvt Ltd
11 Community Centre, Panchsheel Park, New Delhi – 110 017, India
Penguin Group (NZ)
67 Apollo Drive, Rosedale, North Shore 0632, New Zealand
(a division of Pearson New Zealand Ltd)
Penguin Books (South Africa) (Pty) Ltd
24 Sturdee Avenue, Rosebank, Johannesburg 2196, South Africa
Penguin Books Ltd, Registered Offices: 80 Strand, London, WC2R 0RL, England

First published by Penguin Group (Australia), 2011

10 9 8 7 6 5 4 3 2 1

Text copyright © Indira Naidoo 2011
Photographs copyright © Alan Benson 2011
Illustrations copyright © Indira Naidoo 2011

The moral right of the author has been asserted

Cover and text design by Kirby Armstrong © Penguin Group (Australia)
Design coordination by Emily O'Neill © Penguin Group (Australia)
Photography by Alan Benson
Propping and styling by Katie Quinn Davies, Sarah O'Brien and Sophie Geoghegan
Typeset in Chaparral Pro by Post Pre-Press Group, Brisbane, Queensland
Colour reproduction by Splitting Image Colour Studio Pty Ltd, Clayton, Victoria
Printed in China by South China Printing Co. Ltd.

National Library of Australia
Cataloguing-in-Publication data:

Naidoo, Indira.
The edible balcony : how to grow fresh food in a small space plus 60 inspiring recipes / Indira Naidoo.
9781921382536 (pbk.)
Includes bibliographical references and index.
Balcony gardening. Cooking.

635.9671

penguin.com.au